*Advance Praise for*

# Capoeira, Black Males, and Social Justice

"In this book, Vernon 'Leão Preto' Lindsay asks the Capoeira community to expand the roda to influence social justice movements. This is a must-read for Capoeiristas doing work in schools."

—Mestre Acordeon, United Capoeira Association

"Once again, Vernon C. Lindsay has taken bold steps to articulate the physical, mental, and spiritual stamina needed to survive and thrive in uncertain times. His ability to reframe the concept of traditional K–12 physical education for Black youth is noteworthy in a time when physical education is slowly being removed from school curriculum. Such a claim to the necessity of physical education should be considered part and parcel of the process to affirm the humanity of Black youth."

—David Stovall, Professor of Educational Policy Studies and African American Studies, University of Illinois at Chicago

"This book, like the author, is innovative. Vernon C. Lindsay offers Ginga as a creative approach for academicians and practitioners to use in their work with Black males."

—Tony Laing, Director of Men of Color Initiative, University of Wisconsin Oshkosh

# Capoeira, Black Males, and Social Justice

**GLOBAL
INTERSECTIONALITY
OF EDUCATION, SPORTS,
RACE, AND GENDER**

Billy Hawkins
*General Editor*

Vol. 1

---

The Global Intersectionality of Education, Sports, Race, and Gender series
is part of the Peter Lang Education list.
Every volume is peer reviewed and meets
the highest quality standards for content and production.

---

PETER LANG
New York • Bern • Berlin
Brussels • Vienna • Oxford • Warsaw

Vernon C. Lindsay

# Capoeira, Black Males, and Social Justice

## A Gym Class Transformed

PETER LANG
New York • Bern • Berlin
Brussels • Vienna • Oxford • Warsaw

Library of Congress Cataloging-in-Publication Data

Names: Lindsay, Vernon C., author.
Title: Capoeira, Black males, and social justice: a gym class transformed /
Vernon Lindsay.
Description: New York: Peter Lang, 2019.
Series: Global intersectionality of education, sports, race, and gender; Vol. 1
ISSN 2578-7713 (print) | ISSN 2578-7721 (online)
Includes bibliographical references and index.
Identifiers: LCCN 2018058155 | ISBN 978-1-4331-6084-4 (hardback: alk. paper)
ISBN 978-1-4331-6590-0 (paperback: alk. paper) | ISBN 978-1-4331-6045-5 (ebook pdf)
ISBN 978-1-4331-6046-2 (epub) | ISBN 978-1-4331-6047-9 (mobi)
Subjects: LCSH: African American boys—Education.
Culturally relevant pedagogy—United States.
Critical pedagogy—United States.
Capoeira (Dance)
Lindsay, Vernon C.
Classification: LCC LC2731 .L55 2019 | DDC 371.829/96073—dc23
LC record available at https://lccn.loc.gov/2018058155
DOI 10.3726/b15204


Bibliographic information published by **Die Deutsche Nationalbibliothek.**
**Die Deutsche Nationalbibliothek** lists this publication in the "Deutsche
Nationalbibliografie"; detailed bibliographic data are available
on the Internet at http://dnb.d-nb.de/.

# CONTENTS

# PREFACE—MY CAPOEIRA STORY

The 45th President of The United States is the embodiment of the systemic problems that prevent America, "from being great again." In his first two years of office, we have witnessed foreign debates via twitter, government shutdowns, and actions aligned with the support of Neo-Nazi hate groups. This text is not about Trump or his administration, but it does reflect the efforts of a school that aimed to equip their students with the tools necessary to resist White supremacy (racism) during the end of Obama's terms in office and the election of the current president. Through a culturally responsive curriculum and the African Brazilian martial art called Capoeira, this book explores how students were encouraged to develop positive self-awareness and discover the courage to influence changes in their communities. It is my belief, supported by the observation of the racist, xenophobic, misogynistic platform that propelled the new Commander in Chief to office, that this is the time to use culturally responsive curricula and creative tools such as Capoeira to encourage social movements led by our youth with the intention to achieve justice for all oppressed people. I intend to give voice to the experiences of Black males in an elementary school and discuss how they, other young people, and adults can work together to influence social justice.

My connection to the African Brazilian martial art of Capoeira that combines music, dance, acrobatics, ritual, and self-defense began when I was a child. During my humble beginnings on the Southside of Chicago in the Chatham community, I enjoyed breakdancing and fighting. I remember attempts to showcase my limited breakdancing skills for my sisters and their friends on a carpeted floor in my childhood home. As the only boy with five sisters, I also remember the joy of spending time with other boys my age and play fighting until someone got hurt or upset. I wasn't formally exposed to Capoeira as a child, but its basic elements of dance and fighting were essential to my upbringing.

As discussed in my first book, *Critical Race and Education for Black Males: When Pretty Boys Become Men*, I grew up in a home with limited resources for extracurricular activities. My father worked as a minister and provided the sole income for my five siblings and me. We took advantage of government resources to pay for groceries. My sisters and I wore clothes from the thrift store. I didn't grow up poor, but as a family with six children living on one income, we had just enough to cover our major expenses. When I was a child, I liked to fight, but martial arts classes were not an option. Although my environment and peers changed when my family moved from the city to the south suburbs, my parents' fixed budget determined other priorities for my siblings and me.

As a PK (preacher's kid) I spent more time than I desired at church. Every Wednesday and Sunday, I was required to attend the church my father pastored in the Roseland community on Chicago's Southside. It was our obligation as PKs to often also spend Saturday mornings at the church to participate in additional religious activities. When we vacationed, we didn't go to theme parks. We went to church conventions so my father could fulfill his leadership responsibilities. I often detested the formality of church and found ways to resist which included fighting with other boys my age in the bathrooms or other places where I could avoid the eyes of adults.

Many years after the Sunday morning brawls ceased, I was introduced to Capoeira in a community not too far from my childhood home. As a recent graduate from the University of Illinois at Chicago who majored in African-American studies and earned a Liberal Arts and Sciences degree, I worked for a non-profit organization when I received a flyer that advertised Capoeira classes. The classes were offered at the 95th and State street fieldhouse in Abbot Park. Because of the class' proximity to where I worked and lived, I decided it was a good idea to stop one evening on the way home.

It was then in the fall of 2006, that my journey as a Capoeirista (a person who trains Capoeira) began. I went to the Abbot Park fieldhouse after work where I found a student of Mestra (Master Teacher) Marisa named Tinta Forte teaching a group of about ten Capoeiristas. They trained a series of movements that sparked memories of breakdancing on the carpeted floor in my parents' home and play fighting with my friends. I was baited by the strength and finesse required to perform Capoeira's physical movements and later hooked by the stories of how enslaved Africans used it to fight for freedom.

In the pages that follow, I offer insight into thirteen years of my experiences in Capoeira as a student, teacher, and entrepreneur on a mission to improve the lives of young people from underserved communities. This book focuses on young Black males during the 2015–2016 academic year, where I was responsible for an after-school program located at an independent private school in Chicago, identified in the text as Marcus Chavez Elementary. I discuss how multiple theories informed pedagogical and research approaches with Capoeira, combined with the school's efforts to support the development of students' critical consciousness and influence racial injustices proved valuable to make an impact in the lives of Black boys. This work also illustrates how the Capoeira program evolved from a gym class to a limited liability company working with multiple individuals and institutions.

A collective effort is required to achieve freedom in the twenty-first century. It will take teachers, students, administrators, activists, politicians, and others aligned with creating a more equitable society to make the necessary changes in the United States. We will need to use our talents, gifts, skills, muscles, and creativity to make the dream of a more equal society a reality. Through the words, sentences, and paragraphs of this book, my overarching goal is to provide you with useful tools to engage in important actions with young people that can increase opportunities for justice, success, and fulfillment.

Vernon C. Lindsay, PhD
Coolidge, Antigua and Barbuda, WI
January 26, 2019

For Capoeira instructional videos, merchandise, and other resources visit:
www.vlindsayphd.com/capoeira

# ACKNOWLEDGMENTS

As with everything that requires self-discipline, creativity, and consistency I must begin these acknowledgments by recognizing The Creator who instilled in me the ability to achieve this goal. Similar to my first book, this work pushed me beyond my misconceived physical and mental limitations. I am grateful for every experience that placed this product in your hand.

Gabriella, Vizuri, Emery, and Mkazo thank you for putting up with my early morning writing sessions, berimbau jam sessions, batizado travels, kitchen kicks, living room flips, and everything else that has been part of my experiences in Capoeira. I love you and thank you for your support.

Thank you, Mestre Acordeon, for endorsing this book and challenging my ideas throughout the writing process. I appreciate you and the United Capoeira Association's community of schools created with the visions of Mestre Rã, and Mestra Suelly. You welcomed me at a time that I did not have a home in Capoeira, and I remain humbled by your teachings and guidance to become the Capoeirista I am today.

I also want to thank Mestre Calango for moving to Chicago, teaching me, and helping form UCA Chicago. Your assistance in the formative years of an phenomenal group of children and adult students was incredible, and it is important that I acknowledge your valuable contributions to the content of this book.

Thank you, Gabi, David, Camile, Tony, and Elizabeth for making the time in your schedules to read drafts of these chapters and provide me with editorial feedback. Your support of this process came at a perfect time, and I want to thank you again for your encouragement, advice, and insights.

Although we have separated and traveled down separate paths to explore the depths of Capoeira, it is imperative that I recognize Professor Tinta Forte and Mestra Marisa. Together you created the foundation of my journey to understand Capoeira. You served as my first teachers, and I want to thank you again for exposing me to this ancient art form. There is nothing but love and respect for you and your work with the Capoeira community in Chicago.

Thank you, Dr. Billy Hawkins and Peter Lang Press for lending your support of this book from the first proposal draft. I look forward to working with you again.

I must acknowledge the support of Jared "Lenhador" Ramer. Jared donated his time and talents to assist with data collection for this study. Thank you for interviewing students, observing classes, housing Mestre, and being a supporter of this work.

Last but not least, I must acknowledge the outstanding team of educators, students, and administrators from the research site of this book. This study would not have been possible without you. Thank you for supporting me, my family, and the vision for Capoeira. Much love to the Capoeirista, Verde, for holding the classes down during me and Mestre Calango's transitions to other responsibilities. I wish you and the school much success in your continued growth as a dynamic community committed to social justice education.

# INTRODUCTION

When I began Capoeira, I did not understand it as a martial art that combines elements of acrobatics, dance, self-defense movements, music, and rituals. My first observation of a class left me confused. To me Capoeira resembled a sacred marriage between martial arts and breakdancing. I was unaware of Capoeira's origins among enslaved people from multiple African countries. How *Capoeiristas* endured persecution in Brazil and yet Capoeira matured through displaced persons around the world was a complete mystery to me. To date, I have studied Capoeira for thirteen years, and it remains a challenge to capture its unique characteristics and influences.

In 2005, I earned a Bachelor's degree from the University of Illinois at Chicago. I majored in African-American Studies, minored in Political Science, and took courses that explored the experiences of the African diaspora and the oppressive societies where many Black people live today. While I had interests in Pan-Africanism and the different experiences of African people around the world, somehow Brazil and Capoeira were not mentioned in my courses or independent studies.

Immediately following graduation from college, I worked at a Starbucks' coffee shop. I needed to make money and the part-time job Starbucks offered me, covered expenses until I found a position aligned with my degree. After approximately three months of fulfilling coffee orders, I found work as a case manager with Metropolitan Family Services where I served as a resource for Hurricane Katrina evacuees. While employed at Metropolitan Family Services, a friend gave me a flyer for a Capoeira class offered at the local park district's fieldhouse.

After work one evening in 2006, my journey with Capoeira began. I attended my first class. I introduced myself to the teacher, Tinta Forte (Capoeira nickname meaning *painted strength*), who belonged to Mestra (Master teacher) Marisa's Cordão de Ouro school. Tinta Forte served as a guide through the labyrinth of this ancient art form; he was the first of many to repeat the dominant narrative of Capoeira's roots in Africa and growth among enslaved Africans in Brazil. The brief introduction to Capoeira's history resonated with me. With each class, I believed my ears heard the voices of my ancestors beckoning me to train harder. My first class was the start of a thirteen-year journey to answer the research question for this book; how can Capoeira encourage meaningful relationships and engage conversations with young Black males to support self-love, community awareness, and activism?

At the heart of the research question that guides this book is providing young people with encouragement and tools that can help them to reach their full potential. This idea that Black boys and other young men of color can do more when they strive for greatness aligned with their unique talents, skills, and abilities inspired the program described in this text. Black boys and other young men of color deserve the opportunity to become their best selves. Creating environments that prepare them to become socially conscious, courageous, and intelligent individuals and members of communities is important work.

## Brazil and United States' Tragedies

A brief exploration of European colonialism's (e.g., racism, White supremacy) role in shaping the history of Capoeira is central to the context of this study. Without the participation of Portugal in the colonization efforts of the African continent, it is not likely that Capoeira would exist in its current form. Similar to Christopher Columbus who is inaccurately associated with discovering America, Pedro Álvares Cabral from Portugal is reported as the sailor who found Brazil (Greenlee, 2016; Metcalf, 2005; Morison,

1993; Skidmore, 1999; Zinn, 1999). Without regard for the native inhabitants of the Americas, Columbus and Cabral made land declarations on the behalf of European expansionism. In reality, the land discoveries were a mistake they exploited while attempting to establish an expedited trade route to India.

As the abundance of resources in Africa and the perceived open terrains of North and South America were identified by Europeans, a colonialization agenda developed that included the exploitation of land, labor and natural resources. Historians suggest that Portugal was the first European nation to establish itself in the continent of Africa (Birmingham, 1999; Frank 1992; Spencer, 1974). Birmingham (1999) argues that the Portuguese efforts to expand rule were in part due to its status as an impoverished nation among other European powers. This lack of status among other countries encouraged expeditions to acquire gold, grains and other items of value. Guided by the desire for power, respect, and White supremacist ideologies Portugal made its way down the West African coast capturing Africans and eventually transporting them as cargo to present day South America.

Many comparisons have been made between the institutions of slavery that empowered the colonization of the Americas. Tannebaum (1992), Elkins (1963), Kolchin (1982), Smedley and Smedley (2012) are among the researchers who have conducted comparative studies with insights into the enslavement of Africans in North and South America. Beginning in 1440 Portugal established itself within the West African coastline as a slave trader (Smedley & Smedley, 2012). According to one 18th century estimate 3,325,000 Africans managed to survive the journey to Brazil, whereas only 420,000 lived through the horrific Middle Passage to chattel slavery in the United States (Curtin,1972). For more than twenty years after the legal end of slavery in the United States, Brazil's institution of forced labor continued until 1888.

To maximize the potential for established social and economic institutions, Africans were added to the slavery force and worked alongside native peoples (Metcalf, 2005). The enslavement of Tupi, Guarani, Gê, Arawak, First Nation People, and Africans was justified under the beliefs that it was necessary for economic stability and that non-Europeans were racially inferior (Du Bois, 2007; Elbl, 2004; Feagin, 2010, 2016; Franklin & Moss, 2000; Rodrigues & Craig, 2018; Zirin, 2014). Such ideologies influenced the resistance movements in the United States and the development of Capoeira in Brazil.

# Capoeira's Competing Definitions and Vague Origins

Many have attempted to offer a simplistic definition of Capoeira. Scholars and practitioners have described it as an African-Brazilian martial art, dance, national sport, enigmatic cultural practice, ritual, Brazilian battle dance, dance-fight hybrid, and folklore (Almeida, 1986; Cachorro, 2012; Capoeira, 1995, 2002; Essien, 2008; Ickes, 2013; Lewis, 1992; Merrell, 2005; Sterling, 2012; Talmon-Chvaicer, 2008). The Capoeira master responsible for creating one of the first formal academies and a physical education curriculum, Manoel Dos Reis Machado—nicknamed Mestre Bimba, once described Capoeira as treachery (Almeida, 1986). Another notable pioneer within the Capoeira world, Vicente Ferreira Pastinha, Mestre Pastinha, adds, "Capoeira is whatever the mouth eats" (Almeida, 1986 p. 1). Due to Capoeira's fusion of dance, acrobatics, self-defense, music, philosophy, competing histories, and rituals it can be difficult to offer a singular encompassing definition.

There also exists debate over the birthplace of Capoeira with some crediting the African continent and others Brazil or Portugal. Scholar T. J. Deschi Obi suggests Capoeira, initially called Engolo, derived from the Bantu speaking peoples of Southern Angola (Deschi Obi, 2008). Greg Downey of Grupo de Capoeira Angola Pelourinho argues Capoeira developed from an African dance called N'golo or Dance of the Zebra practiced in Angola (Downey, 2005). Through the identification of Portuguese terms for movements, musical instruments, and Catholic symbols in Capoeira, some offer Brazil and Portugal as possible origins (Burt & Butler, 2011; Lewis, 1992; Merrell, 2005). Others argue that Capoeira is a combination of physical movements and rituals from multiple countries within the African continent that merged during the colonization of Brazil among people in the *senzalas* or slave quarters (Assunção, 2005, Cachorro, 2012; Capoeira, 1995, 2002; Talmon-Chvaicer, 2008). The roots of Capoeira are African, however, it is important to acknowledge the branches and leaves that sprouted in Brazil.

When referencing Capoeira throughout the text, I am defining it as a martial art that fuses dance, acrobatics, music, self-defense, communal philosophies, and rituals. This definition alongside the belief it was born in Africa among multiple nations and grew up in Brazil, as one of many resistance tools, informs my thesis. These points of origin and definition reflect what I taught my students, including the Black boys who agreed to participate in this study. It is these understandings of Capoeira that led to my initial position as the physical education teacher for the school that later served as the research site.

## Marcus Chavez Elementary

Marcus Chavez Elementary (Pseudonym) is a Chicago area school that stems from an early learning center located in a predominately lower-income community of color. It was created in response to parents' wishes for an extension of the successful infant—preschool education program. At the time of the study for this book, Marcus Chavez Elementary offered a kindergarten—eighth grade education with an optional Gap Year program before graduation to high school. The Gap Year program provided students with another year of classroom instruction alongside community service projects. Many of the students who attended Marcus Chavez Elementary self-identified as either Black or Latino/a.

In ten years, Marcus Chavez Elementary expanded from an early learning childcare facility to a robust school with a mission that included social justice. It took pride in a culturally responsive curriculum that covered the core academic subjects and the physical education program. As the school's first Capoeira teacher, I was largely responsible for forming the physical education curriculum to reflect the students' backgrounds and meet the state standards. Over time, my responsibilities in graduate school and the resources available to Marcus Chavez Elementary changed, which influenced the transition of my role as a full-time physical education teacher to an after-school facilitator.

During the 2015–2016 academic year, I volunteered my time and services to coordinate, research, and guide an after-school initiative that offered Capoeira. Twice a week, I arrived at the school's campus to teach Capoeira to students in grades 5-Gap Year. While there were several students who were familiar with Capoeira due to my previous role in the school, I had the opportunity to expose a new group to physical movements and mental exercises that explored music, history, and philosophy.

## Why Black Boys

Although, I taught students of multiple gender and racial identities while working at Marcus Chavez Elementary, I decided to focus on Black boys in this presentation of the research. This decision was made in part to personal and professional experiences. I grew up with other Black boys who co-conspired to transform schools to theaters where we could perform misguided interpretations of masculinity and lowered academic expectations correlated with perceptions of race. As a father of two Black boys, I also felt a need to understand the potential of Capoeira and other creative resources to make a positive impact in their lives. In my professional experiences in public, charter, and private schools, I have witnessed the use and effectiveness of Capoeira to assist the formation of positive relationships between youth and adults (Lindsay, 2013; 2015, 2018a, 2018b). It is for these reasons and others that the experiences of Black boys are highlighted in this study.

Too often young Black males attend schools that underserve their needs to make a positive transition to adulthood. Some succumb to curricula that is void of relevance to their lives and as such, engage in behaviors that often produce negative consequences. Others do well and develop the academic resilience necessary to persevere and gain employment or other economic opportunities. In the mid-1980s, increased attention to the academic achievement of Black males and correlations with discipline policy began among a community of researchers (Anderson, 1990, 1999; Davis & Jordan, 1994; Fultz & Brown, 2008; Garibaldi, 1986, 2007; Gary, 1981; Johnson, 2010; Laing & Brown, 2017). They were concerned about the relationship between schools and the preparation of Black boys for success in and beyond the classroom.

The inability of many schools to provide Black males with transferable skills to improve their lives has implications visible in report cards and in their communities. Researchers have confirmed that when Black boys fail in school, they also experience economic, health, familial, and a host of other challenges correlated with race, masculinity, and opportunity (Fergus & Noguera, 2010; Gill, 1992; Goldberg, 2013; Howard, 2014; Noguera, 2008; Terry, 2010; Toldson, 2008). In the state of Illinois, a 2009 report (as cited in Freeman & Holton, 2009) indicated noticeable differences between the academic achievements of African American males and other males. According to the data, African American males in Illinois are less likely to complete high school and finish college. This report also confirms that Black males more often experience incarceration, limited financial earnings, more frequent contact with the child welfare system, and a shorter life expectancy due to inadequacies in the education, criminal justice, and healthcare systems.

There are significant challenges in schools that often produce negative outcomes for African American males. In the 2012–2013 academic year,

Black and Latino male students were least likely to graduate from high school in forty-eight states (Beaudry, 2015). Many students of color attend schools with inadequate resources to prepare them for successful community engagement, entrepreneurial, or well-compensated employment opportunities. In response to school shortcomings, some Black males engage in self-defeating resistance behaviors such as dropping out, skipping class, fighting peers, or other activities that jeopardize options available through education. After-school programs designed to encourage healthy lifestyle choices, increase social awareness, provide mentorship, and address racial injustices can make a positive impact in the lives of young Black males.

Through providing Black boys with instruction in Capoeira, I witnessed the influence it had in raising social consciousness and improving academic and social performances in school (Lindsay, 2013, 2018a, 2018b). For some, participation in Capoeira class served as a motivational tool to improve in other subjects and interactions with their peers. There were others who did not connect with Capoeira, however, through interviews and observations I found measurable layers of success to validate it as a tool among others for physical fitness, critical discussions, and actions aligned with social justice. While I had the responsibility of educating boys and girls, my findings indicate my instructional approaches and the subject resonated more with young men. Due to the identified challenges with schools and the potential of young people, it became pertinent to focus on Black boys and highlight the use of Capoeira in assisting them to navigate race, gender, and masculinity.

The options to participate in positive educational activities during and after school is critical to the success of Black males. Prominent researchers of Black males enrolled in K-higher education schools confirm school engagement is often part of the foundation that enables lasting achievements (Harper, 2013; Harper & Quaye, 2007; Howard, 2014; Seligson & MacPhee, 2004). Although I am not affiliated with a Black Greek organization, my dissertation findings report the positive impact they can have on supporting student involvement, building academic resilience, creating transformative resistance, and other factors that influence the trajectories for young Black males (Lindsay, 2013). In many cases, the presence of other Black male administrators, teachers, or researchers in schools can make a measurable impact on the lives of young people (Laing, 2017). There are multiple variables impacting the experiences of Black males in schools and it is possible to provide programming that can increase opportunities for academic and other forms of achievement.

## An Overview of the Text

This book serves three purposes: (1) To shed light on my experiences using Capoeira as a tool to build coalitions with young Black males; (2) To provide teachers with replicable insights to engage students in healthy activities, critical conversations, and strategies to influence social justice; and (3) To offer insight into critical race, culturally responsive, intersectionality, and youth development theories and practices that can improve schools in urban environments. Through extracting data from observations, interviews with students and staff, and samples of teaching artifacts, this book represents a collective effort to instill positive self-awareness, inspire leadership, and encourage discipline among Black boys and other young men of color.

My humble efforts to fulfill this text's objectives begin with the aforementioned research question; how can Capoeira encourage meaningful relationships and engage conversations with young Black males to support self-love, community awareness, and activism? To answer this question, each chapter uses data that illustrates research, activities, and discussions used in a Chicago school to encourage healthy lifestyle choices, develop social consciousness, influence positive self-awareness, and take actions to address injustices. I also discuss how I transitioned from a physical educator to forming a limited liability company that expanded Capoeira classes to multiple communities. Stories extracted from interviews, my teaching journals, field notes, and observations collected during the 2015–2016 academic year are reflected within the findings' chapters of this text.

In each chapter, including this introduction, I use the following markers to reference myself, subject participants, and others when applicable: Black, male, African-American, African in America, person of African descent, boy, and man. Through my transition from adolescent to adult, I have resonated with the terms Black man, male, boy, a person of African descent, and an African in America to reflect my racial identity, gender, and ancestral lineage. I am inclined to use Black, because it indicates identity for people born throughout the African diaspora. Male is a biological term that is declared in reference to genital assignment at birth.

There are multiple ways that others may choose to define their identities including bi-racial, mixed, fluid, or transgender. Some elect to use the pronouns "him," "he," or "his" to reference themselves and others with a preference for "they." I understand the complexity of identity and throughout the chapters, I do my best to represent the experiences of others who self-identi-fied their race and gender.

Chapter 1, *Ginga, Black Males, and Education*, illustrates a history of Black males in education, an analysis of contemporary factors impacting K–12 schools, and the multi-theoretical framework that influenced this research. This chapter begins with a reference to learning the foundational movement of Capoeira and drawing a correlation with the beginning of slavery in the United States. I discuss how the formative years of education in the United States impacted the limited opportunities available to Black males. It continues with a discussion of some of the significant themes sur-rounding the literature on African American boys in education with insight to how theories and practices help make meaning of K–12 experiences in school.

Chapter 2, *Documenting Black Males to Understand Pedagogy and Poten-tial*, discusses the data collection methods informed by critical race theory, auto ethnography, and action research used in this study. I articulate how qualitative inquiry helped place race and gender at the center of a study designed to investigate the impact of Capoeira on the lives of students. In detail, I share how field notes of participatory observations, journal entries, and interviews were collected. Overall, this chapter describes how other researchers can duplicate similar studies with young people enrolled in urban schools.

Chapter 3, *From Gym Class to the Community*, uses my teaching jour-nal entries and field notes to explain how a gym class expanded to include an after-school program. Through the narrative expressed in this chapter, I share how Capoeira class began at Marcus Chavez Elementary and over time became a limited liability company. I discuss how from an open house pro-posal, I became the physical education teacher. This chapter discusses how the United Capoeira Association supported my role and encouraged me to explore the depth of Capoeira. The chapter is structured to demonstrate how conversations with Black males can lead to actions aligned with critical race theory, intersectionality, culturally responsive curriculum, and positive youth development.

Chapter 4, *When Black Males Speak*, extracts interview data collected from the students who participated in the study to give voice to their experiences. It provides the responses gathered from Black boys during individual and focus group interviews. This chapter offers insight into the mental, physical, and socio-emotional benefits, as identified by Black boys, that can accompany the practice of Capoeira. It also demonstrates how after-school programs that use Capoeira can influence students to take actions aligned with social justice.

Chapter 5, *Resistance, School Culture, and Capoeira* shares the story of how Capoeira supported a demonstration to protest a series of police homicides of young people of color throughout the United States. In this chapter, I offer field note observations of a school sponsored march and interview data collected from teachers and administrators. These findings provide insight into the culturally responsive curriculum used at the research site to encourage students' actions to address injustices. I discuss how the curriculum offered during the school day influenced students' receptiveness to Capoeira.

Chapter 6, *Relevance Without Compromise*, discusses how this study fits into broader conversations about culturally responsive physical education curriculum, social justice, and educational policy in the United States. It explores the strengths and weaknesses of this study to investigate strategic improvement for future investigations, curriculum innovations, physical education and after-school programs. In this final chapter, I share the need for teachers and administrators to extend the walls of their classrooms and the paper of standardized tests to make the necessary impact on students of color and their communities.

## Capoeira Beginnings and Black Boy Endings

As indicated in the opening paragraph of this introduction, I was unfamiliar with the history of Capoeira when I saw it for the first time as an adult. Growing up in the United States I did not have opportunities, similar to many Brazilian young people, to see Capoeira in my daily environment. After enrolling in classes and traveling to Brazil with and without my students, I began to think about how Capoeira could help Black boys in their transition from adolescence to adulthood. In the spirit of enslaved Africans, this book provides insight to pedagogy and the potential that Capoeira can release in Black boys to achieve success.

In conducting the research and making progress in my business to share Capoeira with young people, my personal development was at the center of these processes. I had to engage activities that supported positive leadership, meaningful personal relationships, healthy lifestyle choices, diverse and inclusive practices, and specific goals to increase productivity. Examples of such activities included maintaining a consistent exercise schedule, working with other teachers to identify my knowledge gaps, spending time with my family, and developing routines aligned with future objectives. Through my physical, mental, and spiritual journey a goal was revealed to help young Black male students also identify their potential. I believe the conversations I shared with students and the direct actions we took together toward addressing racial injustices was part of a larger life purpose.

Proponents of the notion that we should focus on "All Lives" and not just "Black Lives" might suggest this book is laden with biases. I would like to respond by stating it is important to note that while all lives have value, Black males are more likely victims of homicide and possess limited opportunities in employment and education in the United States (Alexander, 2015; Pratt-Harris, et.al, 2016; Reich, 2017; Smith & Patton, 2016). My awareness of this unfortunate reality compels me to focus on remedies that can impact opportunities available for this population first and foremost. Overall, the text hopes to show how Capoeira and conversations about social inequalities served as the nexus between encouraging participation, inspiring academic success, building relationships with young Black males, and creating strategies to engage social justice.

With the intention to serve as a blueprint for similar programs, this work represents my experiences as an after-school facilitator, researcher, student, mentor, teacher, and businessperson. This book is not an attempt to suggest that the solution to the problems many Black boys encounter can be corrected with one simple adjustment. While I have found Capoeira to be a useful engagement tool to build relationships and organize positive resistance behaviors among Black males, I understand it is one of many resources that can be used in schools. Multiple activities, conversations, and creative outlets will present a more holistic solution to the complex challenges of Black males in US schools. Individual and systemic approaches are necessary to make a lasting impact in the lives of Black boys.

Throughout the book, I illustrate how multiple theoretical frameworks and actions impacted students and influenced the instruction of Capoeira at Marcus Chavez Elementary. Each chapter explores my experiences with Capoeira and Black boys in the US education system. It builds from the premise that every human being, including young Black males possesses the potential to present their best selves to this world.

To view images and other content relative to my work with Capoeira and community empowerment visit: www.vlindsayphd.com/about

# References

Alexander, M. (2015). Foreword. In A. Beaudry (Ed). *Black lives matter: The Schott 50 state report on public education and Black males*. New York, NY: Schott Foundation. Retrieved from www.blackboysreport.org

Almeida, B. (1986). *Capoeira, a Brazilian art form: History, philosophy, and practice*. Berkeley, CA: North Atlantic Books.

Anderson, E. (1990). *Streetwise: Race, class, and change in an urban community*. Chicago, IL: University of Chicago Press.

Anderson, E. (1999). *Code of the street: Decency, violence, and the moral life of the inner city*. New York: W.W. Norton and Company.

Assunção, M. R. (2005). *Capoeira: The history of an Afro-Brazilian martial art*. New York, NY: Routledge.

Beaudry, A. (Ed). (2015, February). *Black lives matter: The Schott 50 state report on public education and Black males*. New York, NY: Schott Foundation. Retrieved from www.blackboysreport.org

Burt, I., & Butler, K. S. (2011). Capoeira as a clinical intervention: Addressing adolescent aggression with Brazilian Martial Arts. *Journal of Multicultural Counseling and Development* 39(1), 48–57.

Cachorro, R. M. (2012). *Unknown Capoeira: Volume two a history of the Brazilian martial art*. Berkeley, CA: Blue Snake Books.

Capoeira, N. (1995). *The little capoeira book*. Berkeley, CA: North Atlantic Books.

Capoeira, N. (2002). *Capoeira: Roots of the dance-fight-game*. Berkeley, CA: Blue Snake Books.

Curtin, P. D. (1972). *The Atlantic slave trade: a census*. Madison, WI: University of Wisconsin Press.

Davis, J. E., & Jordan, W. J. (1994). The effects of school context, structure, and experiences on African-American males in middle and high schools. *Journal of Negro Education, 63*, 570–587.

Deschi Obi, T. J. (2008). *Fighting for honor: The history of African martial art traditions in the Atlantic World*. Columbia, SC: University of South Carolina Press.

Downey, G. (2005). *Learning capoeira: Lessons in cunning from an Afro-Brazilian art*. New York, NY: Oxford University Press.

Du Bois, W. E. B. (2007). *The suppression of the African slave-trade to the United States of America 1638 – 1870*. New York, NY: Cosimo.

Elbl, I. (2004). "Slaves are a very risky business ...": Supply and demand in the early Atlantic slave trade. In C. J. Curto & E. P. Lovejoy (Eds.). *Enslaving connections: Changing cultures of Africa and Brazil during the era of slavery* (pp. 29–56). Almherst, New York: Humanity Books.

Elkins, S. M. (1963). *Slavery: A problem in American institutional and intellectual*. Chicago, IL: University of Chicago Press.

Essien, A. (2008). *Capoeira beyond Brazil: From a slave tradition to an international way of life*. Berkeley, CA: Blue Snake Books.

Feagin, J. R. (2010). *Racist America: Roots, current realities, and future reparations.* New York, NY: Routledge.

Feagin, J. R. (2016). *How Blacks built America: Labor, culture, freedom, and democracy.* New York, NY: Routledge.

Fergus, E., & Noguera, P. (2010). *Theories of change among single-sex schools for Black and Latino boys: An intervention in search of theory.* New York, NY: Metropolitan Center for Urban Education.

Frank, T. (1992). Europe—prelude to expansion. *GeoJournal, 26*(4), 465–469.

Franklin, J. H., & Moss, A. A. (2000). *From slavery to freedom: A history of African Americans.* New York, NY: Knopf.

Freeman, A., & Holton, J. K. (2009). *Causal factors underlying disparities in the condition of African American men in Illinois.* Chicago, IL: Illinois Department of Human Services.

Fultz, M., & Brown, A. (2008). Historical perspectives on African American males as subjects of education policy. *American Behavioral Scientist, 51*(7), 854–871.

Garibaldi, M. A. (1986). Sustaining Black educational progress: Challenges for the 1990s. *Journal of Negro Education, 55*(3), 386–396.

Garibaldi, A. M. (2007). The educational status of African American males in the 21st century. *Journal of Negro Education, 76*(3), 324–333.

Gary, L. (Ed.). (1981). *Black men.* Beverly Hills, CA: Sage.

Gill, W. (1992). Helping African American males: The cure. *The Negro Educational Review, 43*(1–2), 31–36.

Goldberg, J. (2013). A matter of Black lives. *The Atlantic.* September 2015. Retrieved on April 16, 2016 from http://www.theatlantic.com/magazine/archive/2015/09/a-matter-of-black- lives/399386/

Greenlee, W. B. (2016). *The voyage of Pedro Álvares Cabral to Brazil and India.* New York, NY: Routledge.

Harper, S. R., & Quaye, S. J. (2007). Student organizations as venues for Black identity expression and development among African American male student leaders. *Journal of College Student Development, 48*(2), 127–144.

Harper, S. R. (2013). Am I my brother's teacher? Black undergraduates, racial socialization, and peer pedagogies in predominantly White postsecondary contexts. *Review of Research in Education, 37*(1), 183–211.

Howard, T. C. (2014). *Black male (D): Peril and promise in the education of African American males.* New York, NY: Teachers College Press.

Ickes, S. (2013). *African-Brazilian culture and regional identity in Bahia, Brazil.* Gainesville, FL: University Press of Florida.

Johnson, W. E. Jr. (2010). From shortys to old heads: Contemporary social trajectories of African American males across the life course. In Waldo E. Johnson (Ed). *Social work with African American males: Health, mental health, and social policy.* New York, NY: Oxford University Press.

Kolchin, P. (1982). Comparing American history. *Reviews in American History, 10*(4), 64–81.

Laing, T. (2017). Black masculinities expressed through and constrained by brotherhood. *Journal of Men's Studies*, 25(2), 168–197.

Laing, T., & Brown, C. (2017). Constructing spaces for diverse black masculinities in all-male public urban schools. In M. A. Peters, (Ed.), *Encyclopedia of educational philosophy and theory*. Singapore, Singapore: Springer Nature.

Lewis, J. L. (1992). *Ring of liberation: Deceptive discourse in Brazilian Capoeira*. Chicago, IL: University of Chicago Press.

Lindsay, V. (2013). *"They Schools Ain't Teachin' Us:" Black males, resistance, and education at Uhuru High School*. (Doctoral Dissertation) Retrieved from Proquest database. University of Illinois at Chicago.

Lindsay, V. (2015) The class that race built: Putting race at the center of a higher education course to challenge post-racialism in the United States and Brazil. *Journal of Higher Education: Theory and Practice: 15*(7), 11–24.

Lindsay, V. (2018a). *Critical race and education for black males: When pretty boys become men*. New York, NY. Peter Lang Press.

Lindsay, V. (2018b). Roda real talk: A physical education teacher's effort to use the capoeira circle as a tool to encourage critical dialogue. In E. Mendoza, B. Kirshner, & K. Gutiérrez (Eds.), *Power, equity, and (re)design: : Bridging learning and critical theories in learning ecologies for youth* (pp. 77–92). Charlotte, NC: Information Age Press.

Merrell, F. (2005). *Capoeira and candomblé: Conformity and resistance through Afro-Brazilian experience*. Princeton, NJ: Markus Weiner.

Metcalf, A. C. (2005). *Go-betweens and the Colonization of Brazil: 1500–1600*. Austin, TX: University of Texas Press.

Morison, E. S. (1993). *The European discovery of America: Vol 2, the southern voyages A.D. 1492–1616*. New York, NY: Oxford University Press.

Noguera, P. (2008). *The trouble with Black boys and other reflections on race, equity, and the future of public education*. San Francisco, CA: Jossey-Bass.

Pratt-Harris, N. C., Sinclair, M. M., Bragg, C. B., Williams, N. R., Ture, K. N., Smith, B. D., … & Brown, L. (2016). Police-involved homicide of unarmed Black males: Observations by Black scholars in the midst of the April 2015 Baltimore uprising. *Journal of Human Behavior in the Social Environment, 26*(3–4), 377–389.

Reich, M. (2017). *Racial inequality: A political-economic analysis*. Princeton, NJ: Princeton University Press.

Rodrigues, L. L., & Craig, R. (2018). The role of government accounting and taxation in the institutionalization of slavery in Brazil. *Critical Perspectives on Accounting. 57*, 21–38.

Seligson, M., & MacPhee, M. (2004). Emotional intelligence and staff training in after-school environments. *New Directions for Youth Development, 103*, 71–83.

Skidmore, E. T. (1999). *Brazil: Five centuries of change*. New York, NY: Oxford University Press.

Smedley, A., & Smedley, B. D. (2012). *Race in North America: Origin and evolution of a worldview*. Boulder, CO: Westview Press.

Smith, J. R., & Patton, D. U. (2016). Posttraumatic stress symptoms in context: Examining trauma responses to violent exposures and homicide death among Black males in urban neighborhoods. *American journal of orthopsychiatry, 86*(2), 212–223.

Spencer, J. H. (1974). Colonial language policies and their legacies in sub-Saharan Africa. In A. J. Fishman (Ed). *Advances in Language Planning* (pp. 163–176). The Hague, The Netherlands: Mouton.

Sterling, C. (2012). *African roots, Brazilian rites: Cultural and national identity in Brazil.* New York, NY: Palgrave Macmillan.

Talmon-Chvaicer, M. (2008). *The hidden history of capoeira: A collision of cultures in Brazilian battle dance.* Austin, TX: University of Texas Press.

Tannenbaum, F. (1992). *Slave and citizen: The classic comparative study of race relations in the Americas.* Boston, MA: Beacon Press.

Terry, C. L. (2010). Prisons, pipelines, and the president: Developing critical math literacy through participatory action research. *Journal of African American Males in Education, 1*(2), 1–33.

Toldson, I. A. (2008). *Breaking barriers: Plotting the path to academic success for school-age African American males.* Washington, DC: Congressional Black Caucus Foundation.

Zinn, H. (1999). *A people's history of the United States.* New York, NY: Harper Collins.

Zirin, D. (2014). *Brazil's dance with the devil: The world cup, the Olympics, and the fight for democracy.* Chicago, IL: Haymarket Books.

# · 1 ·

# GINGA, BLACK MALES, AND EDUCATION

My first Capoeira class as a student was difficult and fun at the same time! For the life of me, I could not comprehend the core movement of Capoeira called *Ginga*. Ginga which translates from Brazilian Portuguese to English as swing or, as Rohter (2010) notes the ability to walk with pride, is the foundation for Capoeira's self-defense movements. It is comparable to the fighting stance boxers learn to protect their body and to create opportunities for attacking an opponent in the ring. Ginga involves stepping back and forth in a triangular motion while using your arms to protect your head or to strike a target.

Ginga is often the starting point for students, because it assists the establishment of a solid base to transition into more complex self-defense and acrobatic movements. It is through mastering Ginga a person can transition from beginner to a more experienced practitioner of Capoeira. Before I attempted Ginga, I assumed it was easy but I quickly learned it took a lot of practice for effective application. Learning Ginga was the start of my journey down the mental, physical, and spiritual paths to understanding the ancient art form of Capoeira.

Ginga is the first movement I taught students in my physical education classes. Similar to the day I began trying to understand Capoeira and the basics such as Ginga, my first students stumbled and struggled with coordination.

They asked a lot of questions for clarity in developing the right form. Most of my students were born in the United States and did not have the cultural lenses of Brazilian Capoeiristas to explore the dance-fight hybrid elements of the art in their environment. Many of my first students did not know about Capoeira's origins as a tool employed by enslaved Africans to resist Portuguese colonial rule.

In the United States, the systemic oppression of Black males began with slavery and continued through laws and policies to maintain limited access to resources necessary for achievement. This chapter dissects the literature on the experiences of Black males in the United States and their efforts to obtain an education. Similar to the Ginga in Capoeira, which serves as a transition stance to execute other movements, this chapter will function as the historical foundation to establish the need to understand more about Black boys in US schools. It begins by exploring White supremacy and the impact it made on the educational opportunities for enslaved Black males. As the foundation for the remainder of the manuscript, this chapter proceeds to demonstrate contemporary literature themes and theories relative to Black males in K–12 schools and concludes with a discussion of how the existing research impacted my approaches to teaching Capoeira.

## White Supremacy

Some would argue that understanding White supremacy or racism, is critical to unpacking the relationship between race, masculinity, and education. Fuller Jr. (1984) suggests that if you do not understand White supremacy, nothing will make sense to you. White supremacy includes the behaviors, laws, practices, and beliefs that support domination by people self-identified as White. Kunjufu (2005) states White supremacy is at the center of an agenda to prevent success among Black males. White supremacy loses itself within the ideas of individuals and finds home in structured inequalities.

Overt Neo-Nazi groups alongside covert policies and laws that support White dominance over people of color is White supremacy (Gillborn, 2005; hooks, 1989). White supremacy includes the actions and ideas that guided Europeans' decisions to colonize the African continent. It is the force behind what Franz Fanon describes as the colonizers' ability to establish a "reign of terror" (Fanon, 1963, p. 208). White supremacy fueled the exploitation of the land, human labor, and natural resources of Africa that served as a precursor to the enslavement of Africans in North and South America.

In the United States, much of the racism that continues to grow stronger today took root in the nation's foundation of slavery. Although the United States was not the first country to implement a free labor system, it was different because Africans were degraded to property or commodities and regulated as inferior by divine order (Cooper, 2015). Evidence of this claim is available in ideas such as the Great Chain of Being by the Neoplatonist Plotinus that supported ideas of natural selection where Whites were assigned identity status similar to God and Africans delegated to a subhuman species (Smedley & Smedley, 2018). Roberts (2011) argues that race is a political system created to separate people based on perceived biological differences. In alignment with Roberts (2011), I suggest race is part of a political system. It is a social and historical construct based on perceived differences in human bodies.

Within the colonies that became the United States, race served as a marker between the enslaved and free persons. Africans from multiple nations became synonymous with inferiority, slavery and US Black identity. Europeans traded in their ethnic identities of German and English in exchange for White, perceptions of prestige, and power. Furthermore, due to the social and historical origins of race, people who did not neatly fit into the dominant categories of Black or White were categorized according to the current political regime (Adelman, 2003; Henze, Katz, Norte, Sather, & Walker, 2002; Singleton & Linton, 2006). As Omi and Winant (1994) suggest, instability is central to the construct of race which enables groups of people to shift between racial categories. An example of this instability phenomenon is exemplified in how Mexicans were recognized as White until they along with others with connections to Spanish histories became Hispanic in alignment with an invented census category (Dávila, 2008; Rodriguez, 2000). Racism, White supremacy, is a derivative of the invention of race and supports systemic subjugation based on perceived differences in human biology (Bonilla-Silva, 2010). Race and racism excused the exploitation of Africans and empowered open exclusion of Black men from educational resources.

## Black Males and Education

Among slave owners, there was a common fear that education could enable Black people to understand their full potential. Through institutionalized slavery and educational policies guided by racism, enslaved Black males were targets of oppression (Anderson, 1988; Watkins, 2001). Evidence of such claims is found among multiples laws that forbid Africans from access to schools; this is reflective in a transcript from an 1832 congressional meeting:

> We have as far as possible closed every avenue by which light may enter their minds. If we could extinguish the capacity to see the light, our work would be completed; they would then be on the level with the beasts of the field and would be safe. (Fultz & Brown, 2008, p. 857)

Such comments made by then Virginia Congressman Henry Berry indicate an intention to restrict awareness with the goal of maintaining slavery and beliefs of racial inferiority. There was much concern that people of African descent would discover the power within themselves and through literacy strengthen the resistance movement to obtain freedom.

If slavery was not enough to control the African population, other practices were established to instill fear. In addition to restricting access to schools, lynching as a form of justice was among the tactics used to scare Black men from believing in a life outside of slavery (Litwack, 2000). Husbands were separated from their wives and children. Black men who demonstrated exemplary strength or skill were imprisoned like animals and forced to live in barns where they were made into breeders to produce more slaves. Due to fear and hatred inspired by internalized racism, men of African descent were often targets of violent oppression (Ball, 2016; Blackmon, 2008; Hodes, 1993; Spiegal, 1996).

Despite the life-threatening consequences, many Black men did not assume passive roles nor accept the institution of slavery in the United States. Gabriele Prosser and Nat Turner led slave revolts in the 1800s and were among a growing population of Black men desperate to escape the inhumane conditions of plantation life (Du Bois, 2017; Fultz & Brown, 2008; Hart, 1980). The concern that educated Blacks might follow in the footsteps of Prosser and Turner or join the abolitionist movement guided deliberate systemic attempts to prevent access to the tools and conditions conducive to learning.

State legislation prevented enslaved African people from attending schools or meeting in any private spaces with the intention to learn how to read and write. Virginia, South Carolina, Alabama, Louisiana, and other states created laws to forbid Black literacy (Andersen & Collins, 1995). There was concern that Black men, women, and children could become aware of the abolitionist movement and fuel efforts to rebel against American slavery. While in many instances Christianity was among the resources used to pacify Black men, there were some who interpreted the ability to read the Bible as a tool for spiritual liberation. Literacy aligned with the actions that some Black men envisioned as central to escaping White supremacy.

The narrative of Booker T. Washington is representative of the types of actions devised to keep men enslaved and the behaviors he and others adopted to learn despite opposition (Washington, 1995). Washington discusses how he could carry the books of his master's children but was prohibited from reading. He had to teach himself how to read while working next to his stepfather in a salt factory. These lessons began with identifying numbers, and over time Washington became literate with the assistance of his mother. In his struggles to reach Hampton Institute, his narrative also discusses how he bartered his labor for food and slept on the streets. Washington was driven to succeed because compared to other Black males, he believed education could improve his community (Anderson, 1988; Jenkins, 2006; Washington, 1995).

Booker T. Washington's relationship to Whiteness is complex. While his narrative demonstrates the resilience that he endured for access to education, it is also important to recognize how White industrialists used him as an advocate for segregation, vocational education, and limiting other Blacks to higher education resources (Chennault, 2013; Johnson & Watson, 2004; Lewis, 2014). Washington was the leader of a campaign that advocated for self-help and economic development, without an analysis of how race, gender and racism influenced opportunities. His, "pull yourself up by the bootstraps," philosophy is void of critical insight to how many people of African descent did not have bootstraps to pull up; they were poor, racialized, and lacked the systemic support necessary to gain social mobility through education.

Another notable Black man who endured slavery, Frederick Douglass, confirms Washington's account of the challenges to learn and the sacrifices necessary to earn an education. To find alone time to study on the plantation, he risked the consequences of flogging or other more severe forms of physical harm, including death. In Douglass's narrative, he discusses how he learned to read from his White mistress, Mrs. Auld, in secrecy from her husband. When they were discovered by Mrs. Auld's husband he responded with the following words:

> If you give a nigger an inch, he will take an ell. A nigger should know nothing but to obey his master–to do as he is told to do. Learning would spoil the best nigger in the world. Now, said he, if you teach that nigger how to read, there would be no keeping him. It would forever make him unfit to be a slave. (Douglass, 1997, p. 325)

Control, the abuse of power, and racism are clear in Mr. Auld's comments. Mr. Auld was furious because he understood that reading could open doors to awareness and encourage more resistance. Despite the challenges to becoming literate, Douglass resisted through perseverance and proceeded to write three narratives articulating his life's experiences.

It is feasible to draw links that indicate a strong relationship between race, White supremacy, gender, and oppression. Given the history of race, White supremacy, and the systemic restrictions to educate Black males, it is feasible to comprehend how Black boys continue to struggle to find social and economic mobility via education (Madhubuti, 1990; Young, 2004). The education system is not intended to facilitate academic achievement among young Black boys. From the origins of the United States, systemic oppression established the lack of desire to educate Black men.

Beliefs that Black men were primitive beings who possessed the potential to use a form of brute force to free themselves justified the tactics used to maintain control. A significant number of the first enslaved Africans in the United States were men (Jenkins, 2006). The narratives of Washington and Douglass demonstrate the challenges Black men encountered when attempting to learn in environments created and supported by White supremacy.

Throughout history, Black men have found education coupled with resistance to serve as necessary partners in the aspirations of increasing opportunities to live better lives. With the understanding that learning to read in school could enable freedom, enslaved Black men, children, and women risked their lives to obtain access to resources (Payne, 2008; Perry, 2003; Williams, 2005). Washington and Douglass are among a significant group of Black males who found reading and writing as essential skills in the struggle for liberation (Anderson, 1988; Perry, Steele, & Hilliard, 2003). The racism that supported slavery in the United States provides a contextual lens to explore current conditions of Black males and their experiences in K–12 schools.

## Black Males in K–12 Schools

In the mid-1980s, researchers increased their attention to the experiences of Black males in educational settings. Popular deficit language used to describe Black boys in the United States included vocabulary such as, "a dying population," "endangered species," and "at risk," (Bailey, 1983; Fultz & Brown, 2008; Gibbs, 1988; Leavy, 1983; Lindsay, 2018a; Parham & McDavis, 1987; Porter, 1997; Strickland, 1989; Young, 2004). Race, racism, masculinity, academic resilience, school discipline policies, critical pedagogy, African-centered curriculum, extracurricular programs, and familial support were established among other factors that can influence educational and other trajectories among Black males. Although there exists an increase in studies and findings since the 1980s, researchers continue to explore the triumphs and challenges of Black boys in schools. Within the current literature, the goals among some researchers remain to improve the explanation of the structural roots of inequalities with aspirations to understand the branches of social inequalities.

## Race, Racism, and Academic Achievement

Race and racism are influential factors in the education of Black males. Although as established earlier, race is a social, historical, and political construction based on perceived differences in human bodies, it continues to impact the experiences of Black males in K–12 schools. Racism, White supremacy, influences individual beliefs and systemic actions that support discrimination based on the social and material currencies that race produces. The legacy of slavery and the denial of access to resources, that Washington and Douglass experienced, remain part of the foundation of the United States. Black males in K–12 schools are often treated and taught differently because of the low value associated with their lives.

While some Black males can excel in school despite the negative implications associated with their racial identity, others have a difficult time developing the positive self-awareness necessary for academic achievement. Scholars have confirmed that race influences the abilities of some young Black males to succeed in schools, because some may begin to internalize the dominant narrative about their identity during adolescence (Chavous et al., 2003; Davis, 2006; Kunjufu, 2005; Ladson-Billings & Tate, 2017; Madhubuti, 1990; Toldson, McGee, & Lemmons, 2015). In major cities throughout the United States including Chicago where the study for this book takes place, researchers have confirmed that race continues to influence academic achievement among young Black males (Allen, 2015; Dumas & Nelson, 2016; Rogers, Scott, & Way, 2015; Warren, 2017; Young, 2004). Racial identity and the impact of White supremacy is among the multiple layers to peel away in the hope of understanding academic achievement among Black males.

While race and racism influence the academic achievement among Black males, they are not the only factors to analyze when attempting to make a case for educational policy changes. The literature that highlights race and racism is compelling and valid; however, it is important to consider how gender influences males who identify as boys, young men, or other identities. Although race and racism are critical to an analysis of understanding academic achievement among Black males, I believe it is also imperative that we consider the influence of masculinity.

## Black Masculinity

Masculinity is how boys learn the acceptable behaviors to perform as men and survive in society. It is a social and cultural construction of male identity, which includes mutually accepted ways to dress and communicate (Brod & Kaufman, 1994; Davis, 2006; Noguera, 2001). A male's internalized perception of masculinity influences his behavioral choices. Some Black males will interpret masculinity and minority status in alignment with Ogbu's cultural ecological theory (Irving & Hudley, 2008; Ogbu, 1987; Ogbu & Simons, 1998). They can find themselves seeking validation through oppositional beliefs and behavioral performances that other men believe is necessary to gain respect. Examples include but are not limited to, acting violently or aggressively to prove self-worth, playing a passive role in class to avoid being labeled smart by their peers or a problem by the teacher, using profane language to intimidate others, treating girls and women with disrespect, developing an attitude that does not make space for quitting until achievement is earned, and sagging their pants can all serve as forms of resistance against accepted cultural norms.

Given the relationship between race and masculinity, many Black males in K–12 schools are often associated without cause to behaviors that can lead to negative consequences. Scholars note how the premature criminalization of Black males in K–12 schools complicates the impact that education can have in the process to obtain success (Allen & White-Smith, 2014; Davis, 2006; Ferguson, 2001; Parker, 2017; Steele & Aronson, 1995). Black males who are criminalized often embrace toxic masculine behaviors. Consequences include dropping out of high school, getting involved in the underground economy, and engaging in other activities that precede incarceration or premature death.

The literature on masculinity and education demonstrates clear links between social expectations, behavioral performances and academic achievement among Black males. Researchers make a solid case that when young Black males internalize what it means to be a boy or man in society, there is the potential for positive and damaging results in schools. The challenge with the literature on masculinity is that it examines the experiences of students on an individualistic level. It places the blame or praise on social behaviors adopted by individuals without analysis of the structures that often influence the education process for young Black males. As we continue to explore the impact of masculinity constructs, it is imperative to acknowledge the policies, laws, and other structural factors that impact human behaviors.

## School Discipline Policies

The social constructions of race and masculinity influence how teachers and administrators receive Black males. In many instances Black males are often labeled as problems, challenges, and concerns within schools. They are not associated with solutions and are over diagnosed as students with Attention Deficit Hyperactivity Disorder (ADHD), assigned Individualized Education Plans (IEP), and relegated to special education classrooms (Grant, 1992; O'Connor & Fernandez, 2006; Pastor, Reuben, Duran, & Hawkins, 2015; Toldson, 2011; Timimi, 2005). Because low academic and behavior expectations are often assumed about Black males, they are frequent recipients of harsh penalties disguised as school discipline policies.

Multiple studies confirm that Black males are more likely to experience suspensions, expulsions, and other punishments due to some violation of school policy. In the 1980s, research revealed that in New Orleans Black males were found to represent 65% of total suspensions, 80% of all expulsions, 58% of non-promotions, and 45% of school dropouts (Garibaldi, 1986, 2007). A national study that took place from 1991–2005 revealed that Black boys were 330 percent (roughly three times) more likely than White boys to experience harsh school discipline policies (Wallace, Goodkind, Wallace, & Bachman, 2008). Trends continue today that indicate Black males encounter multiple systemic challenges in United States schools.

Harsh school discipline policies are indeed problematic for Black males who attend K–12 schools. Polices with phrases such as "zero tolerance" disproportionately render no tolerance to young Black men who resist policies. I am one of those Black males who did not comply with school policies and as a result, was suspended in middle and high school (Lindsay, 2018a). A discussion of how to create more resilience in response to harsh discipline policies is limited in this body of research. It often highlights problems and does not offer potential remedies.

## Academic Resilience

Despite the challenges of race, racism, masculinity, and school discipline policies, some Black males achieve academic success. The ability to succeed in schools is often related to academic resilience. Academic resilience is the skill to rise above a similar set of challenges that your peers encounter to earn the grades necessary for promotion (Gayles, 2005; Kim & Hargrove, 2013; Rhoden, 2017; Spencer, Fegley, Harpalani, & Seaton, 2004). Black males who embody academic resilience frequently believe in the potential that an education can provide, despite the opposition they face alongside their friends.

Black males who develop the skill of academic resilience can create a positive influence on their future. Researchers have confirmed that Black males who possess academic resilience have more opportunities made available to them (Payne, Starks, & Gibson, 2009; Swanson, Cunningham, & Spencer, 2003; Whiting, 2014). African-American males who allow their grades to suffer, because they have not harnessed the ability to excel when their friends are failing, often do not graduate (Roderick, 2003; White & Rayle, 2007). While researchers note academic resilience as a necessary element to increase opportunities for achievement among Black boys, several factors remain that influence the ability to obtain this vital skill.

Multiple studies confirm the idea that the ability to adopt academic resilient behaviors is a primary factor responsible for grade promotion and can lead to successes outside the school building (Payne et al., 2009; Roderick, 2003; White & Rayle, 2007). The literature on academic resilience is essential in understanding why some Black males perform well in school, but it fails to acknowledge how curriculum discourages duplicate behaviors among others. If the goal is to increase achievement among Black boys, it will require an in-depth analysis of teachers' lesson plans and methodologies to ensure classrooms serve as relevant resources for preparation.

## Critical Pedagogy

Critical pedagogy consists of a structured learning relationship between educators and researchers designed to prepare students for real-world application of knowledge acquired in classrooms. A teacher who uses critical pedagogy should consider how race, racism, masculinity, discipline policies, and academic resilience influences African-American male students. Critical pedagogy is a derivative of philosophies that established the need to use schools as a vehicle to drive change in the social and political environments of their students (Darder, Baltodano, & Torres, 2003; Duncan-Andrade & Morrell, 2008; Freire, 2007; Giroux, 2001; hooks, 1994; Kincheloe, 2005; McLaren & Kincheloe, 2007). Teachers and administrators should support using critical pedagogy to increase chances of success for all students. It has the potential to provide Black male students and others with pathways to the application of their education.

The pioneer in critical pedagogy is the Brazilian philosopher, Paulo Freire. Before his passing in 1997, he documented his experiences as an educator who championed the rights of underserved people. In his famous book, *Pedagogy of the Oppressed*, he discusses the importance of creating educational opportunities that move away from memorization to the concrete application of knowledge. Freire explains, "Liberating education consists in acts of cognition, not transferals of information" (Freire, 2007, p. 79). When administrators fail to encourage teachers to discover methods to make the lessons relevant to the lives of their students beyond high scores on tests, schools disservice young people and limit their potential.

The lack of critical pedagogy in schools is an issue worthy of attention. We need more educators willing to create and teach lessons that prepare young people to respond to the challenges of their communities. In our current schools where standardized tests are often indicators for performance and learning, critical pedagogical educators must resist the "common sense" of teaching to the exam. The research on critical pedagogy highlights why it is a crucial classroom resource. However, there is limited research explaining methods or strategies of implementation.

## African-Centered After-school Programs for Awareness and Achievement

After-school programs structured with an African-centered curriculum is an approach used in some schools to increase academic achievement among Black males. Within this model, educators provide positive representations of African people to connect with their students' histories and build the character necessary for achievement (Astante, 1988; Diop, 1978; Karenga, 1990; Madhubuti & Madhubuti, 1994; Mbiti, 1970; Sofola, 1973; Stuckey, 1987; Warfield-Coppock, 1990). It has the potential to increase the positive self-awareness necessary to acquire academic resilience and understand how to influence teachers' and administrators' interpretations of school policies.

Instead of narrowing the experiences of Black males in the United States to slavery and topical analyses of the civil rights era, teachers who use an African centered curriculum access a longer timeframe and depth of contributions (Lee, 2008; Lee, Lomotey, & Shujaa, 1990). In these programs, students are encouraged to explore a comprehensive history. They work toward a collective understanding of their roles in society and move away from European models of rugged individualism.

An African-centered after-school initiative has the potential to make a positive impact on academic achievement and encourage community engagement activities. The best after-school programs serve as a home for young people to receive mentorship from adults (Hirsch, 2005). Researchers have found that some of the most effective after-school programs for young Black males use materials that encourage positive self-awareness, community improvement initiatives, and promote relationships with older Black men (Butler-Derge, 2009; Kafele, 2009; Kunjufu, 2005; Porter, 1997). Given the work engaged by myself and others using Capoeira as a resource to connect with young people in K–20, and after-school settings, it is possible to witness the benefits of sharing rich traditions created by people of the African diaspora (Burt, 2015; Burt & Butler, 2011; Essien, 2008; Lindsay, 2013, 2015, 2018a, 2018b). The infusion of ideas, concepts, and practices that uplift Black people during an after-school program have the potential to influence youth in their academic pursuits and beyond.

An African-centered after-school program must embody positive values and traditions. This approach can offer opportunities to "develop critical thinking and group protection to bring about self-determination for Black people" (Porter, 1997, p. 66). Through rites-of-passage activities that include meaningful conversations and other tools of engagement, young Black males can explore the concepts of Maulana Karenga's Nguzo Saba principles that encourage unity, creativity, positive self-awareness, and a smooth transition from adolescence to adulthood (Butler-Derge, 2009; Karenga & Karenga, 2007; Kunjufu, 2005). In the same vein, African-centered after-school programs can encourage academic achievement and a broadened view of potential among Black males.

Although there is significant research on the education of Black males in public schools, there is limited research on the variety of identities that Black males can adopt and the potential impact of Africentric programs. African-centered programming and rites-of-passage programs remain criticized for the high values placed upon the Black experience and their lack of attention to participating youth of multiple identities (Banks, 1993; Singer, 1994; Sleeter, 1996). Ginwright (2004) argues that African-centered programs must move beyond an emphasis on West African and ancient Kemetic (Egyptian) history, culture, and values to engage young people of multiple racial and sexual identities, or they will remain limited in the attempt to address the diverse experiences and identities of Black males in K–12 education settings.

## Parental Support

It's important to discuss the impact of family on academic success among Black males. For all students, regardless of race and gender, support at home whether in the form of primary caregivers, grandparents, aunts, uncles, or other parental arrangements is critical to preparation for school achievement (Hill & Taylor, 2004; Jeynes, 2007; Wilder, 2014; Wilson, 1978). When the student is from a lower income community, Clark (1983) argues it is not enough to have a mother or father involved in school activities. He states that they must also possess an optimistic mindset of the outcomes an education can provide and relay them to their children. Research indicates that when parents of Black males are involved in their schooling and express expectations to attend college, it can encourage academic achievement (Harper, 2006, 2010; Jones, Kenyon-Rowan, Ireland, Niehaus, & Skendall, 2012; McDonough, 1997). If college is the goal, then encouragement by parental figures is important for Black male students.

In many schools, some young Black males feel shunned due to established intersections between identity, discipline policies, and the acquisition of tools necessary to achieve. Parents or other supervision figures, who help with homework, provide productive outlets during downtime, can influence and support academic accomplishments among Black males (Bryant, 2000; Donnor, 2006; Mandara, 2006). They can also encourage involvement in extracurricular activities such as sports that can lead to a mixed bag of future opportunities (Comeaux, 2010; Howard, 2014; James, 2016). The impact of an involved parent or family member can counter some of the damage done by the persistence of racism and toxic masculinity.

It is essential to recognize the importance of parental support in the education of Black males. The literature identifies how the possession of an involved mother or father can increase academic performance, extracurricular activity involvement, and perspective changes that can embrace college as a viable option. Black males do not need helicopter parents or parents that hover over every choice. They do not need lawnmower parents or parents that attempt to mow down and eliminate every obstacle. African-American males need supportive families to help them explore the intersections between race, class, gender, and educational opportunities.

It is crucial for Black males to do well in school and produce grades that are reflective of their potential, but the school is not the sole arbiter of achievement. I also suggest that academic achievement begins when the application of ideas discussed in the classroom are applied in students' communities. African-American males and other students must find ways to extract the concepts taught in schools to produce viable solutions toward neighborhood challenges. To bridge the connections between schools and the pavement, theoretical frameworks are necessary for analysis and implementation.

# Theoretical Insights and Practical Visions for Black Males

## Critical Race Theory

Critical race theory is a valuable resource in understanding how race, racism, power, and the property rights of Whiteness influence the experiences of Black boys in K–12 schools. With origins in the 1970s and extractions from critical legal studies that explored inequalities in the legal system, critical race theory offers valid assistance to examine disparities that persist beyond the civil rights era (Corbado, 2011; Crenshaw, 2011; Delgado & Stefancic, 2001; Jennings & Lynn, 2005; Ortiz & Elrod, 2002). Through critiquing the education system and supporting policy, critical race theory in education serves as a theoretical and methodological paradigm to confront racism and the subjugation of people of color (Matsuda, 1995; Solorzano & Bernal, 2001). For Black boys, whose voices are often silenced, critical race theory in education serves as the lever to increase the volume, so their experiences are heard.

In education, critical race theorists illustrate how the permanence of racism, the limited effectiveness of civil rights laws, colorblind ideologies, and the property rights of Whiteness converge to influence school inequalities (Gunby-Decuir, 2006; Harris, 1995, 2001; Ladson-Billings & Tate, 2017). Narratives are used as tools to challenge the authority of the court system, and dominant stories that refuse to address the persistence of White supremacy in the United States and abroad (Bell, 1987, 1992; Delgado & Stefancic, 2001;

Gillborn, 2005; Ladson-Billings & Tate, 2006; Montoya, 2002; Ortiz & Elrod, 2002; Ross, 2002).

Critical race theory has proved valuable in understanding the impact of racialization on marginalized groups of young people in schools. Solorzano and Bernal (2001) provide evidence of the effectiveness of critical race theory in their analysis of Chicano/a students. Beratan (2006) demonstrates the value of critical race theory to make sense of the alarming numbers of children of color labeled as disabled. Others have shown the effectiveness of critical race theory to understand the experiences of Black boys in K–12 schools and colleges (Dixson, 2006; Donnor, 2006; James, 2016).

Although critical race theory is a valuable analytical tool to explain how Black males process the intersections between race, racism, and power, it also has limitations. Some scholars have argued that it is inadequate to explain the nuances of identity, language, immigration concerns, ethnicity, phenotype, and sexuality (Solarzano & Bernal, 2001). Others have claimed that CRT fails to offer a valid critique of liberalism and relies too much on narratives to validate claims of racial inequalities (Farber & Sherry, 2016; Litowitz, 2016). With regards to Black males, critical race theory offers a limited analysis of young people who may identify with multiple racial, sexual, or gender identities. For these critiques and others, some suggest that we must consider various paradigms to understand and respond to the experiences of Black males in K–12 schools.

## Intersectionality Theory

Intersectionality theory is an analytical tool that can assist investigations aimed to offer insight into the relationships between gender, ethnicity, race, sexual identity, class, age, and other social constructs; it provides a powerful lens to begin exploring the experiences of Black males in K–12 schools (Caton, 2012; Collins, 2004; Jean-Marie, Williams, & Sherman, 2009; Thomas & Stevenson, 2009). The documented experiences of women of color who engaged dialogue and other actions consistent with feminist thought formed the intersectionality paradigm to explore how social constructs often operate interdependently and influence people's experiences (Collins, 2000; Glenn, 1998; Murphy, Hunt, Zajicek, Norris, & Hamilton, 2009). In Kimberle Crenshaw's foundational article on the construct of intersectionality, she demonstrates how race and gender influence domestic violence policies and extends to other structural, political, and social implications (Crenshaw,

1995). Consistent with intersectionality, it is feasible to identify how race, age, gender, and sexual identity impact the experiences of Black males in K–12 schools.

Through dominant perspectives of masculinity in a patriarchal society that associate men with power and leadership, in some instances Black males can be perceived as privileged. However, the relationships between race, gender, and other identity markers uniquely shape the benefits and challenges that accompany Black boys and other young men of color (Curry, 2014). Intersectionality helps us understand how choices, outcome, and status in society to converge to influence privilege and oppression. It gives insight to "(1) contextuality and dynamism of intersections, (2) mutual constitution, and (3) matrix of domination" (Murphy et al., 2009, p. 9). While in general, possessing male identity comes with opportunities, the weight of other social constructs influences the experiences of Black males. Intersectionality offers an analysis of the multiple layers that come with identification as a person of color in societies built from the foundations of White supremacy. Intersectionality theory's emphasis on social constructions and experiences is critical to understanding the experiences of Black males in K–12 educational settings.

There exist strengths and weaknesses in the use of intersectionality in making sense of Black male students in K–12 schools. Intersectionality empowers us to investigate how race, gender, class, sexual identity, and age influence individual and systemic oppression. By attempting to assess these social markers simultaneously, we can create policies and culturally responsive curricula that foster more opportunities through education. The challenge with an intersectional analysis to understanding the experiences of Black males in K–12 schools lies in the difficulty in discerning with clarity which construct is the dominating factor worthy of remedies. Policies, curriculum, and after-school initiatives impacting Black males in K–12 schools should be comprehensive and derive from a singular point to encourage a positive transition from adolescence to adulthood.

## Positive Youth Development Theory

Positive youth development theory highlights the importance of empowering young people to reach their potential. Through work in schools, non-profit organizations, after-school programs, churches, mosques, and community centers, positive youth development supports initiatives that bridge gaps between adults and young people (Larson, 2000; Masten, 2014; MacPhee &

Seligson, 2004; Pollack, 2004; Roth, Brooks-Gunn, Murray, & Foster, 1998; Bernstein-Yamashiro, 2004). Positive youth development theory has been instrumental in programs that challenge myths and encourage the aforementioned academic resilience. (Kurtines et al., 2008; Romero & Cammarota, 2009; Roth et al., 1998). It emphasizes strong coalitions that can influence guided trajectories from adolescence to adulthood. For these reasons, it is vital for educators to embrace their roles as influencers within the positive youth development paradigm in relation to Black males in K–12 schools.

Teachers who see themselves as an extension of their students' parents can encourage high academic performance among Black males. Positive youth development theory emphasizes the roles of school teachers in creating productive relationships between students and educational institutions. When Black boys and other young people feel a genuine connection between their teachers, administrators, and other school personnel it can influence life-long learning and healthy transitions from adolescence to adulthood (Milner, 2010; Noam & Fiore, 2004; Pianta, 1999; Pollack, 2004; Roth et al., 1998). Strong coalitions between adults and young people is an overarching theme of much of the research in the field of positive youth development.

In regards to devising solutions to address community challenges, positive youth development reinforces the importance of inclusive approaches that include the voices of adults and young people. Lakes (1996) argues that youth must have full membership in intergenerational alliances to encourage cohesive democratic actions. With the intention to transform lives and communities, Ginwright and Cammarota (2006), offer a three-step social justice youth development model. This social justice youth development model begins with young people adopting and accepting a holistic comprehension of their selves that consider race, class, gender, and sexual identity. It continues with supporting the idea that young people must develop an awareness to understand how inequalities shape their communities. The third and final step of the social justice youth development model encourages the expansion of step two to explore the connection between local, national, and global oppressions.

There are strengths and weaknesses in the field of positive youth development theory to analyze the experiences of Black males in K–12 schools. Positive youth development theory helps us understand how adult and youth coalitions can influence academic success and community engagement. It offers insight to support relationships that can assist Black males to do well in school and inspire service to their neighborhoods. Positive youth development theory does not demonstrate how young people can empower themselves without adults to make productive and positive societal contributions. Unlike critical race theory, the literature of positive youth development does not offer analyses into how race influences relationships and opportunities. With the adoption of the social justice lens that emphasizes self-awareness and social consciousness, positive youth development theory illustrates much potential in understanding more about how to help Black male students.

## Culturally Responsive Physical Education

Culturally responsive curriculum in the core academic subjects including physical education aims to increase academic achievement and create social awareness with the intention to disrupt the status quo (Ladson-Billings, 1995; Lindsay, 2018b). This pedagogical approach to teaching, learning, and designing curriculum values the cultural lenses that frame how students see the classroom. Culturally responsive curriculum highlights students' native languages, familial backgrounds, communities, racial, gender, and other identities as assets with the intention to create a critical analysis of knowledge (Gay, 2000; Ladson-Billings, 2009). It is a useful tool in math, science, English, social studies, art, gym, and other classes that can influence Black males' preparation for success (Thomas & Warren, 2017).

A culturally responsive physical education curriculum (CPRE) extracts ideas, concepts, and pedagogical approaches from a culturally responsive curriculum in the core academic subjects and applies it to physical education (Lindsay, 2018b). Students' socially constructed identities, including race and gender, are made integral to discovering physical activities that support healthy lifestyles in spaces that support culturally responsive physical education curricula (Young & Sternod, 2011). This approach of making the students' identities integral to instruction is consistent with a culturally responsive curriculum in other school subjects. CRPE can serve as a partner to remedies such as obesity and unsafe environments that often plague underserved communities of color (Shaibi, Ball, & Goran, 2006; Suarez-Balcazar, Friesema, & Lukyanova, 2013; Fawcett & Barroso, 2010; Lindsay, 2018b; Scott, Lee, Lee, & Kim, 2006; Harrolle, Floyd, Casper, Kelley, & Bruton, 2013). When Black males and other students can see themselves in their teachers' lesson plans, they are more likely to develop a more invested interest in the topic and to discover how the subject applies to their lives beyond the walls of the school building.

Teachers equipped with the strategies and tools to teach students from diverse populations can influence the success of culturally responsive physical education programs. To assess pedagogical practices in Southwestern US' school districts with 50,000 students, Culp and Chepyator-Thomson (2011) utilized the Infusing Multicultural Physical Education Attitudes in Curriculum for Teachers (IMPACT) survey. The IMPACT survey measured how the teachers' beliefs of culturally responsive curricula influenced implementation. One significant finding of the study indicated that some physical education teachers believe they are not provided with adequate training to ensure quality instructional methods with culturally responsive curricula. Such inadequacies become intensified when White teachers are asked to implement a curriculum designed to meet the needs of students of color.

Some benefits and challenges can accompany the use of culturally responsive physical education programs designed to impact the experiences of Black males in K–12 schools. CRPE can encourage healthy lifestyle choices, improve academic performance, and participation in social justice initiatives. They can also influence some Black boys to seek validation through physical achievements in sports activities or what others have recognized as athletic seasoning complex (Edwards, 2000; Eitle & Eitle, 2002; Harris, 2012; Howard, 2014; Lindsay, 2018a). Culturally responsive physical education programs are important and if used in alignment with their strengths and weaknesses can improve the lives of Black boys in K–12 schools.

## Conclusion: Back to Ginga

Research demonstrates the complexity of understanding how to release the full potential of Black males in K–12 schools throughout the United States. Young African-American boys are an extension of the experiences that Washington and Douglass described as part of the challenges they encountered for access to an education. Such factors that influence contemporary education challenges include the dominant narratives Black males internalize, the acquisition of academic resilience, school discipline policies, pedagogical approaches, extracurricular programs, and familial support. Critical race theory, positive youth development, and culturally responsive physical education curriculums can offer insight into useful theories and methods for improving the life choices of Black males in K–12 schools. With these understandings, I chose Capoeira to encourage relationships, mentor young Black males, and encourage engagements in community initiatives.

When I started to teach Capoeira, I approached my job at Marcus Chavez Elementary internalizing this chapter's explanations of White supremacy, the history of Black males in education, contemporary factors influencing K–12 experiences, and the potential of the identified theoretical frameworks. As the physical education teacher at Marcus Chavez Elementary, I felt compelled to develop exercises for the students' minds and bodies. Together we explored history, physical movements such as Ginga, the percussion instruments, and rituals of Capoeira.

# References

Adelman, L. (2003). *Race: The power of an illusion* (Video). San Francisco, CA: Newsreel/PBS.

Allen, Q. (2015). "I'm Trying to Get My A": Black male achievers talk about race, school and achievement. *The Urban Review, 47*(1), 209–231

Allen, Q., & White-Smith, K. A. (2014). "Just as bad as prisons": The challenge of dismantling the school-to-prison pipeline through teacher and community education. *Equity & Excellence in Education, 47*(4), 445–460.

Anderson, J. D. (1988). *The education of blacks in the South, 1860–1935*. Chapel Hill, NC: The University of North Carolina Books.

Andersen, M., & Collins, H. P. (Eds.). (1995). *Race, class and gender* (2nd ed.). Belmont, CA: Wadsworth.

Asante, M. (1988). *Afrocentricity*. Trenton, NJ: Africa World Press.

Bailey, P. (1983, August). A manchild of the 80s: Boys meet the challenge of growing up in Harlem, U.S.A. *Ebony*, 68–72.

Banks, J. (1993, September). Multicultural education: Development, dimensions and challenges. *Phi Delta Kappan, 75*(1), 22–28.

Ball, E. L. (2016). The politics of pain: Representing the violence of slavery in American Popular Culture. In D. Schmid (Ed.), *Violence in American Popular Culture* (pp. 27–44). Santa Barbara, CA: ABC-Clio, LLC.

Bell, D. (1987). *And we are not saved: The elusive quest for racial justice*. New York, NY: Basic Books.

Bell, D. (1992). *Faces at the bottom of the well: The permanence of racism*. New York, NY: Basic Books.

Bell, D. (2005). Who's afraid of critical race theory? In R. Delgado & J. Stefancic (Eds.), *The Derrick Bell reader* (pp. 78–84). New York, NY: New York University Press.

Beratan, G. D. (2006). Institutionalizing inequity: Ableism, racism and IDEA 2004. *Disability studies quarterly, 26*(2)

Bernstein-Yamashiro, B. (2004). Learning relationships: Teacher-student connections, learning, and identity in high school. *New Directions for Youth Development, 2004*(103), 55–70.

Blackmon, D. A. (2008). *Slavery by another name: The re-enslavement of black Americans from the Civil War to World War II*. New York, NY: Anchor Books.

Bonilla-Silva, E. (2010). *Racism without racists: Color-blind racism and the persistence of racial inequality in the United States.* Lanham, MD: Rowman & Littlefield.

Brod, H., & Kaufman, M. (Eds.). (1994). *Theorizing masculinities.* Thousand Oaks, CA: Sage Publications.

Bryant, N., Jr. (2000). African American males: Soon gone? *Journal of African American Men, 4*(4), 9–17.

Burt, I. (2015). Transcending traditional group work: Using the Brazilian martial art of capoeira as a clinical therapeutic group for culturally diverse adolescents. *The Journal for Specialists in Group Work, 40*(2), 187–203.

Burt, I., & Butler, K. S. (2011). Capoeira as a clinical intervention: Addressing adolescent aggression with Brazilian Martial Arts. *Journal of Multicultural Counseling and Development, 7*(3), 249–261.

Butler-Derge, S. (2009). *Rites of passage: A program for high school African American males.* Lanham, MD: University Press of America.

Caton, M. T. (2012). Black male perspectives on their educational experiences in high school. *Urban Education, 47*(6), 1055–1085.

Chavous, T. M., Bernat, D. H., Schmeelk Cone, K., Caldwell, C. H., Kohn Wood, L., & Zimmerman, M. A. (2003). Racial identity and academic attainment among African American Adolescents. *Child Development, 74*(4), 1076–1090.

Chennault, R. (2013). Pragmatism and progressivism in the educational thought and practices of Booker T. Washington. *Philosophical Studies in Education, 44*, 121–131.

Clark, R. (1983). *Family life and school achievement: Why poor black children succeed or fail.* Chicago, IL: University of Chicago Press

Collins, H. P. (2000). *Black feminist thought: Knowledge, consciousness, and the politics of empowerment* (2nd ed.). New York, NY: Routledge.

Collins, H. P. (2004). *Black sexual politics: African Americans, gender and the new racism.* New York, NY: Routledge.

Cooper, I. (2015). Commodification of the Black Body, Sexual Objectification and Social Hierarchies during Slavery. *Earlham Historical Journal,* (pp. 21 – 43)

Comeaux, E. (2010). Academic engagement of black male student athletes: Implications for practice in secondary and postsecondary schooling. In W. E. Johnson (Ed.), *Social work with African American males: Health, mental health, and social policy* (pp. 147–161). New York, NY: Oxford University Press.

Corbado, D. W. (2011). Critical what? *Connecticut Law Review, 34*(5), 1595–1643.

Crenshaw, W. K. (1995). Mapping the margins: Intersectionality, identity politics, and violence against women of color. In W. K. Crenshaw, N. Gotanda, G. Peller, & K. Thomas (Eds.), *Critical race theory: The key writings that formed the movement* (pp. 357–383). New York, NY: The New Press.

Crenshaw, W. K. (2011). Twenty years of critical race theory: Looking back to move forward. *Connecticut Law Review, 43*(5), 1255–1346.

Culp, B., & Chepyator-Thomson, J. R. (2011). Examining the culturally responsive practices of urban primary physical educators. *Physical Educator, 68*(4), 234–253.

Curry, T. J. (2014). Michael Brown and the need for a genre study of black male death and dying. *Theory & Event, 17*(3). Darder, A., Baltodano, M., & Torres, R. D. (2003). *The critical pedagogy reader.* New York, NY: Routledge Falmer.

Dávila, A. (2008). *Latino spin: Public image and the Whitewashing of race.* New York, NY: New York University Press.

Davis, J. E. (2006). Research at the margin: Mapping masculinity and mobility of African-American high school dropouts. *International Journal of Qualitative Studies in Education, 19*(3), 289–305.

Davis, J. E., & Jordan, W. J. (1994). The effects of school context, structure, and experiences on African American males in middle and high school. *The Journal of Negro Education, 63*(4), 570–587.

Delgado, R. (2000). Storytelling for oppositionists and others: A plea for narrative. In R. Delgado & J. Stefancic (Eds.), *Critical race theory: The cutting edge* (pp. 60–70). Philadelphia, PA: Temple University Press.

Delgado, R., & Stefancic, J. (2001). *Critical race theory: An introduction.* New York, NY: New York University Press.

Delgado, R., & Stefancic, J. (2000). *Critical race theory: The cutting edge.* Philadelphia, PA: Temple University Press.

Diop, C. (1978). *The cultural unity of Black Africa.* Chicago, IL: Third World Press.

Dixson, A. D. (2006). The fire this time: Jazz, research and critical race theory. In A. D. Dixson & C. K. Rousseau (Eds.), *Critical race theory in education: All God's children got a song* (pp. 213–232). New York, NY: Routledge.

Donnor, K. J. (2006). Parent(s): The biggest influence in the education of African American football student-athletes. In A. D. Dixson & C. K. Rousseau (Eds.), *Critical race theory in education: All God's children got a song* (pp. 153–166). New York, NY: Routledge.

Douglass, F. (1997). Narrative of the life and times of Frederick Douglass. In L. H. Gates, Jr., & N. Y. McKay (Eds.), *The Norton anthology: African American literature* (pp. 299–400). New York, NY: W. W. Norton.

Du Bois, W. E. B. (Ed.). (2017). *Black reconstruction in America: Toward a history of the part which black folk played in the attempt to reconstruct democracy in America, 1860–1880.* Routledge.

Dumas, J. M., & Nelson, D. J. (2016). (Re)imagining black boyhood: Toward a critical framework for educational research. *Harvard Educational Review, 86*(1), 27–47.

Duncan-Andrade, M. R., & Morrell, E. (2008). *The art of critical pedagogy: Possibilities for moving from theory to practice in urban schools.* New York, NY: Peter Lang.

Essien, A. (2008). *Capoeira beyond Brazil: From a slave tradition to an international way of life.* Berkeley, CA: Blue Snake Books.

Fanon, F. (1963). *The wretched of the earth.* New York, NY: Grove Press.

Farber, A. D., & Sherry, S. (2016). Telling stories out of school: An essay on legal narratives. In E. Taylor, D. Gillborn, & G. Ladson-Billings (Eds.), *Foundations of critical race theory in education* (pp. 310–333). New York, NY: Routledge.

Fawcett, K. A., & Barroso, I. (2010). The genetics of obesity: FTO leads the way. *Trends in Genetics, 26*(6), 266–274.

Ferguson, A. A. (2001). *Bad boys: Public schools in the making of black masculinity*. Ann Arbor, MI: University of Michigan Press.

Freire, P. (2007). *Pedagogy of the oppressed* (30th ed.). New York, NY: Continuum.

Fuller, N. Jr. (1984). *The united independent compensatory code/system/concept: A textbook/workbook for thought, speech, and/or action for victims of racism (White supremacy)*. Washington, D.C.: Nfj Productions.

Fultz, M., & Brown, A. (2008). Historical perspectives on African American males as subjects of education policy. *American Behavioral Scientist, 51*(7), 854–871.

Garibaldi, M. A. (1986). Sustaining black educational progress: Challenges for the 1990s. *Journal of Negro Education, 55*(3), 386–396.

Garibaldi, M. A. (2007). The educational status of African American males in the 21st century. *Journal of Negro Education, 76*(3), 324–333.

Gay, G. (2000). *Culturally responsive teaching: Theory, research, and practice*. New York, NY: Teachers College Press.

Gayles, J. (2005). Playing the game and paying the price: Academic resilience among three high-achieving African American males. *Anthropology & Education Quarterly, 36*(3), 250–264. Retrieved from http://dx.doi.org/10.1525/aeq.2005.36.3.250

Gibbs, J. T. (1988). *Young, black and male in America: An endangered species*. New York, NY: Auburn House.

Gillborn, D. (2005). Education policy as an act of White supremacy: Whiteness, critical race theory and education reform. *Journal of Education Policy, 20*(4), 485–505.

Ginwright, S. A. (2004). *Black in school: Afrocentric reform, urban youth & the promise of hip-hop culture*. New York, NY: Teachers College Press.

Ginwright, S. A., & Cammarota, J. (2006). Introduction. In S. A. Ginwright, P. Noguera, & J. Cammarota (Eds.), *Beyond resistance! Youth activism and community change: New democratic possibilities for practice and policy for America's youth* (pp. xiii–xxii). New York, NY: Routledge.

Giroux, H. A. (2001). *Theory and resistance in education: Towards a pedagogy for the opposition* (Rev. ed.). Westport, CT: Bergin & Garvey.

Glenn, N. A. (1998). The social construction and institutionalization of gender and race: An integrative framework. In M. N. Ferree, J. Lorber, & B. Hess (Eds.), *Revisioning gender* (pp. 3–43). Thousand Oaks, CA: Sage.

Gunby-Decuir, T. J. (2006). Proving your skin is White, you can have everything: Race, racial identity and property rights in Whiteness in the Supreme Court case of Josephine Decuir. In D. A. Dixson & C. K. Rosseau (Eds.), *Critical race theory in education: All God's children got a song* (pp. 89–112). New York, NY: Routledge.

Grant, P. (1992). Using special education to destroy black boys. *Negro Educational Review, 43*(1), 17–21.

Harper, P. M. (1996). *Are we not men? Masculine anxiety and the problem of African American identity*. New York, NY: Oxford University Press.

Harper, S. R. (2006). Reconceptualizing reactive policy responses to black male college achievement: Implications from a national study. Retrieved from http://repository.upenn.edu/gse_pubs/169

Harper, S. R. (2008). The effects of sorority and fraternity membership on class participation and African American student engagement in predominantly White classroom environments. *College Student Affairs Journal*, 27(1), 94–115.

Harper, S. R. (2010). An anti-deficit achievement framework for research on students of color in STEM. *New Directions for Institutional Research*, 2010(148), 63–74.

Harper, S. R., & Harris, F. (2006). The role of Black fraternities in the African American male undergraduate experience. In M. J. Cuyjet (Ed.), *African American men in college* (pp. 129–153). San Francisco, CA: Jossey-Bass.

Harper, S. R., & Quaye, S. J. (2007). Student organizations as venues for black identity expression and development among African American male student leaders. *Journal of College Student Development*, 48(2), 127–144.

Harris, A. P. (2001). Foreword. In R. Delgado & J. Stefancic (Eds.), *Critical race theory: An introduction* (pp. xvii–xxi). New York, NY: New York University Press.

Harris, C. I. (1995). Whiteness as property. In K. Crenshaw, N. Gotanda, & K. Thomas (Eds.), *Critical race theory: The key writings that formed the movement* (pp. 276–291). New York, NY: New Press.

Harris, P. C. (2012). The sports participation effect on educational attainment of black males. *Education and Urban Society*, 46(5), 507–521.

Harrolle, M. G., Floyd, M. F., Casper, J. M., Kelley, K. M., & Bruton, C. M. (2013). Physical activity constraints among Latinos: Identifying clusters and acculturation differences. *Journal of Leisure Research*, 45(1), 74–90.

Hart, R. (1980). *Slaves who abolished slavery: Blacks in rebellion* (vol. 2). Barbados: University of West Indies Press.

Henze, R., Katz, A., Norte, E., Sather, S., & Walker, E. (2002). *Leading for diversity: How school leaders promote positive interethnic relations*. Thousand Oaks, CA: Corwin Press.

Hill, N. E., & Taylor, L. C. (2004). Parental school involvement and children's academic achievement: Pragmatics and issues. *Current directions in psychological science*, 13(4), 161–164.

Hirsch, B. J. (2005). *A place to call home: After-school programs for urban youth* (1st ed.). Washington, D.C. & New York, NY: American Psychological Association and Teachers College Press. Retrieved from http://www.loc.gov/catdir/toc/ecip0421/2004018838.html

Hodes, M. (1993). The sexualization of reconstruction politics: White women and black men in the South after the Civil War. *Journal of the History of Sexuality*, 3(3), 402–417. Retrieved from http://www.jstor.org/stable/3704014

hooks, b. (1989). *Talking back: Thinking feminist, Thinking black*. Cambridge, MA: South End Press.

hooks, b. (1994). *Teaching to transgress: Education as the practice of freedom*. New York, NY: Routledge.

Howard, T. C. (2014). *Black male(d): Peril and promise in the education of African Americanmales*. New York, NY: Teachers College Press.

Irving, A. M., & Hudley, C. (2008). Oppositional identity and academic achievement among African-American males. In J. U. Ogbu (Ed.), *Minority status, oppositional culture, & schooling* (pp. 374–394). New York, NY: Routledge.

James, E. C. (2016). Why is the school basketball team predominately black? In E. Taylor, D. Gillborn, & G. Ladson-Billings (Eds.), *Foundations of critical race theory in education* (pp. 63–76). New York, NY: Routledge.

Jean-Marie, G., Williams, V. A., & Sherman, S. L. (2009). Black women's leadership experiences: Examining the intersectionality of race and gender. *Advances in Developing Human Resources, 11*(5), 562–581.

Jenkins, T. S. (2006). Mr. Nigger: The challenges of educating Black males within American society. *Journal of Black Studies, 37*(1), 127–155.

Jennings, E. M., & Lynn, M. (2005). The house that race built: Critical pedagogy, African-American education, and the re-conceptualization of a critical race pedagogy. *Educational Foundations, 19*(3–4), 15–32.

Jeynes, W. H. (2007). The relationship between parental involvement and urban secondary school student academic achievement: A meta-analysis. *Urban Education, 42*(1), 82–110.

Johnson, K. V., & Watson, E. (2004). The WEB DuBois and Booker T. Washington Debate: Effects upon African American Roles in Engineering and Engineering Technology. *Journal of Technology Studies, 30*(4), 65–70.

Jones, R. S., Kenyon-Rowan, T. H., Ireland, S. M., Niehaus, E., & Skendall, C. K. (2012). The meaning students make as participants in short term immersion programs. *Journal of College Student Development, 53*(2), 201–220.

Kafele, B. K. (2009). *Motivating black males to achieve in school and in life.* Alexandria, VA: ASCD.

Karenga, M. (1990). *The Book of coming forth by day: The ethics of the declaration of the innocence.* Los Angeles, CA: University of Sankore Press.

Karenga, M., & Karenga, T. (2007). The nguzo saba and the black family: Principles and practices of well-being and flourishing. In H. P. McAdoo (Ed.), *Black Families* (pp. 7–28). Thousand Oaks, CA: Sage Publications.

Kim, E., & Hargrove, D. T. (2013). Deficient or resilient: A critical review of Black male academic success and persistence in higher education. *The Journal of Negro Education, 82*(3), 300–311.

Kincheloe, J. (2005). *Critical pedagogy.* New York, NY: Peter Lang.

Kunjufu, J. (2005). *Countering the conspiracy to destroy black boys* (vol. 1, 2nd ed.). Chicago, IL: African American Images.

Kurtines, M. W., Wreder-Ferrer, L., Berman, L. S., Lorente, C. C., Silverman, K. W., & Montgomery, J. M. (2008). Promoting positive youth development: New directions in developmental theory, methods, and research. *Journal of Adolescent Research, 23*(3), 233–244.

Ladson-Billings, G. (1992). Reading between the lines and beyond the pages: A culturally relevant approach to literacy teaching. *Theory Into Practice, 31*(4), 312–320.

Ladson-Billings, G. (2009). *The dream-keepers: Successful teachers of African American Children.* San Francisco, CA: Jossey-Bass.

Ladson-Billings, G. (1995). Toward a theory of culturally relevant pedagogy. *American Educational Research Journal, 32*(3), 465–491.

Ladson-Billings, G., & Tate, W. F. (Eds.). (2006). *Education research in the public interest: Social justice, action, and policy.* New York, NY: Teachers College Press

Ladson-Billings, G., & Tate, W. F. (2017). Toward a critical race theory of education. In *Critical race theory in education* (pp. 11–31). New York, NY: Routledge.

Lakes, R. D. (1996). *Youth development and critical education*. Albany, NY: State University of New York Press.

Larson, R. W. (2000). Toward a psychology of positive youth development. *American Psychologist, 55*(1), 170–183. doi:10.1037/0003-066X.55.1.170

Leavy, W. (1983, August). Is the Black male an endangered species? *Ebony*, 41–46.

Lee, C. D. (2008). Profile of an independent black institution: African centered education at work. In M. C. Payne & C. S. Strickland (Eds.), *Teach freedom: Education for liberation in the African-American Tradition* (pp. 208–221). New York, NY: Teachers College.

Lee, C. D., Lomotey, K., Shujaa, M. (1990). How shall we sing our sacred song in a strange land? The dilemma of double consciousness and the complexities of an African-centered pedagogy. *Journal of Education, 172*(2), 45–61.

Lewis, T. (2014). Booker T. Washington's audacious vocationalist philosophy. *Oxford Review of Education, 40*(2), 189–205.

Lindsay, V. (2015). The class that race built: Putting race at the center of a higher education course to challenge post-racialism in the United States and Brazil. *Journal of Higher Education: Theory and Practice, 15*(7), 11–23.

Lindsay, V. (2013). *"They Schools Ain't Teachin Us": Black males, resistance, and education at Uhuru High School* (Doctoral Dissertation). Retrieved from Proquest database. University of Illinois at Chicago.

Lindsay, V. (2018a). *Critical race and education for black males: When pretty boys become men*. New York, NY: Peter Lang Press.

Lindsay, V. (2018b). Roda real talk: A teacher's effort to use the capoeira circle as a tool to encourage critical dialogue. In E. Mendoza, B. Kirshner, & K. Gutiérrez (Eds.), *Power, equity, and (re)design: Bridging learning and critical theories in learning ecologies for youth* (pp. 77–92). Charlotte, NC: Information Age Press.

Litwack, F. L. (2000). *Without sanctuary: Lynching photography in America*. Santa Fe, NM: Twin Palms.

Litowitz, E. D. (2016). Some critical thoughts on critical race theory. In E. Taylor, D. Gillborn, & G. Ladson-Billings (Eds.), *Foundations of critical race theory in education* (pp. 293–309). New York, NY: Routledge.

Lynn, M. (1999). Toward a critical race pedagogy: A research note. *Urban Education, 33*(5), 606–626.

MacPhee, M., & Seligson, M. (2004). Emotional intelligence and staff training in after school environments. *New Directions for Youth Development*, (103), 71–83.

Madhubuti, H. R. (1990). *Black men obsolete, single, dangerous? The African American family in transition*. Chicago, IL: Third World Press.

Madhubuti, H. R., & Madhubuti, S. (1994). *African-centered education: Its value, importance, and necessity in the development of black children*. Chicago, IL: Third World Press.

Mandara, J. (2006). The impact of family functioning on African American males' academic achievement: A review and clarification of the empirical literature. *Teachers College Record, 108*(2), 206–223.

Matsuda, M. (1995). Critical race theory and critical legal studies: Contestation and coalition. In K. Crenshaw, N. Gotanda, G. Peller, & K. Thomas (Eds.), *Critical race theory: The key writings that formed the movement* (pp. 63–79). New York, NY: The New Press.

Mbiti, J. (1970). *African religion and philosophy*. New York, NY: Anchor Books.

McDonough, P. M. (1997). *Choosing colleges: How social class and schools structure opportunity*. Albany, NY: State University of New York Press.

McLaren, P., & Kincheloe, L. J. (Eds.). (2007). *Critical pedagogy: Where are we now?* New York, NY: Peter Lang.

Masten, A. S. (2014). Invited commentary: Resilience and positive youth development theory frameworks in developmental science. *Journal of Youth and Adolescence, 43*(6), 1018–1024.

Milner, R. H. (2010). *Start where you are, but don't stay there: Understanding diversity, opportunity gaps, and teaching in today's classrooms*. Cambridge, MA: Harvard Education Press.

Montoya, E. M. (2002). Celebrating racialized legal narratives. In F. Valdes, J. M. Culp, & P. A. Harris (Eds.), *Crossroads, directions and a new critical race theory* (pp. 243–250). Philadelphia, PA: Temple University Press.

Murphy, Y., Hunt, V., Zajicek, N. A., Norris, A. N., & Hamilton, L. (2009). *Incorporating intersectionality in social work practice, research, policy and evaluation*. Washington, D.C.: National Association of Social Workers Press.

Noam, G. G., & Fiore, N. (2004). Relationships across multiple settings: An overview. *New Directions for Youth Development, 2004*(103), 9–16.

Noguera, P. (2001, December 1). Joaquin's dilemma: Understanding the link between racial identity and school-related behaviors. *Motion Magazine*. Retrieved from http://www.inmotionmagazine.com/er/pnjoaq1.html

Noguera, P. (2008). *The trouble with black boys: Essays on race, equity, and the future of public education* (1st ed.). San Francisco, CA: Jossey-Bass.

O'Connor, C., & Fernandez, S. D. (2006). Race, class, and disproportionality: Reevaluating the relationship between poverty and special education placement. *Educational Researcher, 35*(6), 6–11.

Ogbu, J. U. (1987). Variability in minority school performance: A problem in search of an explanation. *Anthropology & Education Quarterly, 18*(4), 312–334.

Ogbu, J. U., & Simons, H. D. (1998). Voluntary and involuntary minorities: A cultural ecological theory of school performance with some implications for education. *Anthropology & Education Quarterly, 29*(2), 155–188.

Omi, M., & Winant, H. (1994). *Racial formation in the United States: From the 1960s to the 1990s*. New York, NY: Routledge.

Ortiz, V., & Elrod, J. (2002). Construction project: Color me queer + color me family = Camilo's story. In F. Valdes, J. M. Culp, & A. P. Harris (Eds.), *Crossroads, directions, and a new critical race theory* (pp. 258–273). Philadelphia, PA: Temple University Press.

Parham, T., & McDavis, R. (1987). Black men, an endangered species: Who's really pulling the trigger? *Journal of Counseling and Development, 66*(1), 24–27.

Parker, L., & Lynn, M. (2002). What's race got to do with it? Critical race theory's conflicts with and connections to qualitative research methodology and epistemology. *Qualitative Inquiry, 8*(1), 7–22.

Parker, L. (2017). Schools and the no-prison phenomenon: Anti-blackness and secondary policing in the black lives matter era. *Journal of Educational Controversy, 12*(1), 1–24.

Pastor, P. N., Reuben, C. A., Duran, C. R., & Hawkins, L. D. (2015). Association between diagnosed ADHD and selected characteristics among children aged 4–17 years: United States, 2011–2013. NCHS Data Brief. Number 201. *Centers for Disease Control and Prevention.*

Payne, C. (2008). Introduction. In M. C. Payne & C. S. Strickland (Eds.), *Teach Freedom: Education for Liberation in the African-American Tradition* (pp. 1–11). New York, NY: Teachers College.

Payne, A. Y., Starks, C. B., & Gibson, R. L. (2009). Contextualizing black boys' use of a street identity in high school. *New Directions for Youth Development, 2009*(123), 35–51.

Perry, T. (2003). Up from the parched earth: Toward a theory of African-American achievement. In T. Perry, C. Steele, & A. III. Hilliard (Eds.), *Young gifted and black: Promoting high achievement among African-American students* (pp. 1–10). Boston, MA: Beacon Press.

Perry, T., Steele, C., & Hilliard, A. III. (Eds.). (2003). *Young gifted and Black: Promoting high achievement among African-American Students.* Boston, MA: Beacon Press.

Pianta, R. (1999). *Enhancing relationships between children and teachers.* Washington, D.C.: American Psychological Association.

Pollack, W. S. (2004). Parent-child connection: The essential component for positive youth development and mental health, safe communities and academic achievement. *New Directions for Youth Development, 2004*(103), 17–30.

Porter, M. (1997). *Kill them before they grow: Misdiagnosis of African American boys in American classrooms.* Chicago, IL: African American Images.

Rhoden, S. (2017). "Trust me, you are going to college": How trust influences academic achievement in Black males. *The Journal of Negro Education, 86*(1), 52–64.

Roberts, D. (2011). *Fatal invention: How science, politics, and big business re-create race in the twenty-first century.* New York, NY: The New Press.

Roderick, M. (2003). What's happening to the boys? Early high school experiences and school outcomes among African American male adolescents in Chicago. *Urban Education, 38*(5), 538–607.

Rodriguez, C. E. (2000). *Changing race: Latinos, the census, and the history of ethnicity in the United States.* New York, NY: New York University Press.

Rogers, L. O., Scott, M. A., & Way, N. (2015). Racial and gender identity among black adolescent males: An intersectionality perspective. *Child Development, 86*(2), 407–424.

Rohter, L. (2010). *Brazil on the rise: The story of a country transformed.* New York, NY: Palgrave Macmillan.

Romero, F. A., & Cammarota, J. (2009). A social justice epistemology and pedagogy for Latina/o students: Transforming public education with participatory action research. *New Directions for Youth Development, 2009*(123), 53–65.

Roth, J., Brooks-Gunn, J., Murray, L., & Foster, W. (1998). Promoting healthy adolescents: Synthesis of youth development program evaluations. *Journal of Research on Adolescence, 8*(4), 423–459.

Ross, T. (2002). The unbearable Whiteness of being. In F. Valdes, J. M. Culp, & A. P. Harris (Eds.), *Crossroads, directions, and a new critical race theory* (pp. 251–257). Philadelphia, PA: Temple University Press.

Scott, D., Lee, S., Lee, J. J., & Kim, C. (2006). Leisure constraints and acculturation among Korean immigrants. *Journal of Park and Recreation Administration, 24*(2), 63–86.

Shaibi, G. Q., Ball, G. D., & Goran, M. I. (2006). Aerobic fitness among Caucasian African-American and Latino youth. *Ethnicity & Disease, 16*(1), 120–125.

Singer, A. (1994, December). Reflections on multiculturalism. *Phi Delta Kappan, 76*(4), 284–288.

Singleton, E. G., & Linton, C. (2006). *Courageous conversations about race: A field guide for achieving equity in schools.* Thousand Oaks, CA: Corwin Press.

Solorzano, D., & Bernal, D. D. (2001). Examining transformational resistance through a critical race and LatCrit theory framework Chicana and Chicano students in an urban context. *Urban Education, 36*(3), 308–342.

Sleeter, C. (1996). *Multicultural education as social activism.* Albany, NY: State University of New York Press.

Smedley, A., & Smedley, B. D. (2018). *Race in North America: Origin and evolution of a worldview.* New York, NY: Routledge.

Sofola, J. A. (1973). *African culture and the African personality.* Ibadan, Nigeria: African Resources.

Spencer, B. M., Fegley, S., Harpalani, V., & Seaton, G. (2004). Understanding hypermasculinity in context: A theory-driven analysis of urban adolescent males' coping responses. *Research in Human Development, 1*(4), 229–257.

Spiegel, M. (1996). *The dreaded comparison: Human and animal slavery.* New York, NY: Mirror Books.

Steele, C. M., & Aronson, J. (1995). Stereotype threat and the intellectual test performance of African Americans. *Journal of personality and social psychology, 69*(5), 797–811.

Strickland W. (1989, November). Our men in crisis: together we must meet the enormous challenge facing Black men. *Essence,* 49–52.

Stuckey, S. (1987). *Slave culture: Nationalist theory and the foundations of black America.* New York, NY: Oxford University Press.

Suarez-Balcazar, Y., Friesema, J., & Lukyanova, V. (2013). Culturally competent interventions to address obesity among African American and Latino children and youth. *Occupational Therapy in Healthcare, 27*(2), 113–128.

Swanson, D. P., Cunningham, M., & Spencer, M. B. (2003). Black males' structural conditions, achievement patterns, normative needs, and "opportunities." *Urban Education, 38*(5), 608–633.

Thomas, D. E., & Stevenson, H. (2009). Gender risks and education: The particular classroom challenges for urban low-income African American boys. *Review of research in education, 33*(1), 160–180.

Thomas, E. E., & Warren, C. A. (2017). Making it relevant: How a black male teacher sustained professional relationships through culturally responsive discourse. *Race Ethnicity and Education, 20*(1), 87–100.

Timimi, S. (2005). *Naughty boys: Anti-social behaviour, ADHD and the role of culture.* New York, NY: Palgrave Macmillan.

Toldson, I. A. (2011). Editor's comment: How black boys with disabilities end up in honors classes while others without disabilities end up in special education. *The Journal of Negro Education*, 80(4), 439–443.

Toldson, I. A., McGee, T., & Lemmons, B. P. (2015). Reducing suspensions by improving academic engagement among school-age black males. In D. J. Losen (Ed.), *Closing the school discipline gap: Equitable remedies for excessive exclusion* (pp. 107–117). New York, NY: Teachers College Press.

Wallace, Jr., J. M., Goodkind, S., Wallace, C. M., & Bachman, J. G. (2008). Racial, ethnic, and gender differences in school discipline among U.S. high school students: 1991–2005. *The Negro educational review*, 59(1–2), 47–62.

Washington, B. T. (1995). *Up from slavery*. Toronto, Ontario, Canada: Dover.

Watkins, H. W. (2001). *The White architects of Black education: Ideology and power in America, 1865–1954*. New York, NY: Teachers College Press.

Watson, E., & Elwood, W. (2004). The W. E. B. DuBois and Booker T. Washington debate: Effects upon African American roles in engineering and engineering technology. *Journal of Technology Studies*, 30(4), 65–70.

Warfield-Coppock, N. (1990). *Afrocentric theory and applications: Afrocentric rites of passage* (vol. 1). Washington, D.C.: Baobab Associates.

Warren, C. (2017). *Urban preparation: Young black men moving from Chicago's south side to success in higher education*. Cambridge, MA: Harvard Education Press.

White, N., & Rayle, D. A. (2007). Strong teens: A school based small group experience for African American males. *The Journal for Specialists in Group Work*, 32(2), 178–189.

Whiting, G. (2014). The scholar identity model: Black male success in the K–12 Context. In F. A. Bonner II (Ed.), *Building on resilience: Models and frameworks of Black male success across the P-20 pipeline* (pp. 88–108). Sterling, VA: Stylus Publishing, LLC.

Wilder, S. (2014). Effects of parental involvement on academic achievement: A meta-synthesis. *Educational Review*, 66(3), 377–397.

Williams, D. R. (2005). The health of U.S. racial and ethnic populations. *The Journals of Gerontology*, 60B(2), 53–62.

Wilson, A. N. (1978). *The developmental psychology of the black child*. New York, NY: Africana Research Publications.

Young, A. A. (2004). *The minds of marginalized Black men: Making sense of mobility, opportunity and future life chances*. Princeton, NJ: Princeton University Press.

Young, S., & Sternod, B. M. (2011). Practicing culturally responsive pedagogy in physical education. *Journal of Modern Education Review*, 1(1), 1–9.

# · 2 ·

# DOCUMENTING BLACK MALES
# TO UNDERSTAND PEDAGOGY
# AND POTENTIAL

In 2015, I worked as a Postdoctoral Fellow in Teaching and Mentoring with the University of Illinois at Chicago's Honors College. I taught undergraduate students in courses that included, *Honors 123: Race, Racism, Power, and Education in the United States* and *Honors 127: The Art of Human Expression in the United States and Brazil.* My classes used critical race theory and Capoeira to discuss the intersections between education, young people, social constructs, inequalities, and political movements. In addition to encouraging life-long learning in the classroom, I conducted the research for this study.

While working at the University of Illinois at Chicago, I also served as the managing owner of a limited liability company. The business started in response to my work as a physical education teacher at Marcus Chavez Elementary and its primary activity involved teaching Capoeira to young people and adults. My company was not compensated for conducting this research or facilitating the after-school program. To prevent a conflict of interest between my research responsibilities and services to the school, I donated my time. One of my adult students, who participated in my business services, was also enrolled at the University of Illinois at Chicago and volunteered to assist with collecting data.

A grant did not fund this study. My assistant and I offered our time, skills, and talents, out of a shared curiosity of how Capoeira and the curriculum at Marcus Chavez Elementary interacted to produce socially aware young people. The lack of funding to support this work did limit our availability at the research site; however, we collected enough data and influenced the problem that inspired this study.

Many of the twenty-one young people who participated in the after-school program were also my students when I served as their physical education teacher at Marcus Chavez Elementary. Although the structure and time for Capoeira class evolved since the full-time position I held in graduate school, the goals to encourage social awareness and build strong relationships with the young people remained the same. Through the critical race, culturally responsive, and positive youth development lenses which support the analysis of race, pedagogy reflective of students' backgrounds, and methods to build coalitions between young people and adults, this Capoeira program became a robust complement, among other activities, aligned with the school's social justice mission. This chapter is intended to provide a detailed account of methods used in this study to help other researchers produce similar research.

## Critical Race, Auto-ethnographic, and Action Research Methods

As discussed in the previous chapter, when critical race theory intersects with education it creates a helpful analytical tool to explore how race, racism, power, and the property rights of Whiteness influence social inequalities. Critical race theory is also a valuable methodological resource that encourages researchers to observe, analyze, and take actions aligned with addressing injustices. There exist five essential components of critical race theory methodology according to Solórzano and Yosso (2016) and cited by Bradley (2009). Critical race theory:

a. Acknowledges the intercentricity of racialized oppression- the layers of the subordination based on race, gender, class, immigration status, surname, phenotype, accent, and sexuality. This intercentricity of race can assist in searching for answers related to the experiences of people of color;

b. Challenges the dominant ideology by challenging White privilege; it rejects the notions of a neutral researcher or objective researchers and

exposes deficit informed research that silences and distorts epistemolo-
gies of people of color;

c. Is committed to social justice, leading to outcomes that eliminate racism, sexism, and poverty, and empowers subordinated minority groups
d. Centers experiential knowledge, recognizing the experiential knowledge of people of color is legitimate, appropriate and critical to understanding, analyzing and teaching about racial subordination;
e. A transdisciplinary perspective, one that insists on analyzing race and
   racism by placing them in both historical and contemporary contexts.
   (Bradley, 2009, p. 67)

This understanding of a, "commitment to social justice," informed my
approach to using methods that corresponded with highlighting the voices
of students of color. My goals as a researcher included extracting critical race
informed data and pouring in positive self-awareness to students in preparation to work together to achieve social justice. In alignment with critical race
methodology and intersectionality theory, I placed race and other factors such
as gender and age at the center of my approach to collect data.

It was my goal as a researcher to discuss and gather data of conversations
that explored the intersections between race, gender, and age. Critical race
theorists do not assume an objective stance in research. They forefront the
narratives of people of color and approach their work through interpreting
the past and present implications of race and other social constructs in the
production and maintenance of inequalities. Scholars note the effectiveness
of critical race methodological approaches in conducting research with Black
males in educational settings (Duncan, 2002, 2005; Harper, 2009; Howard,
2008; Stovall, 2006; Tate, 1997).

In addition to critical race methods, I also approached this study guided by
principles consistent with auto-ethnographies. Auto-ethnographies explore
inquiries by using journals, artifacts, clothing, architecture, texts, movies,
photographs, and video recorded observations (Camangian, 2010; Ellis,
Adams, & Bochner, 2010; Goodall, 2006; Neumann, 1999; Thomas, 2010).
They have served as valuable research and analytical tools in classrooms,
community centers, and after-school programs (Duncan, 2002; Gatson, 2011;
Hamilton, Smith, & Worthington, 2008; Rodriguez-Valls, 2016). Alongside
the social justice emphasis of critical race methods, the auto-ethnographic
approach enabled me to understand how my experiences as a person of color
shaped data collection.

As the facilitator of the after-school program, it was impossible to teach and simultaneously take note of my practices and the students' behaviors. Methods consistent with auto-ethnographies enabled me to assess data after each classroom observation and session of the after-school program. Although my role in the Capoeira program included facilitating and investigating, I also approached the work with an intention to be mindful of the needs of my students. This required me to drop my goals of attempting to make meaning of every interaction with the students and remain present to the moment. Auto-ethnographic methods offered me valuable tools to interpret pedagogy and gather data from video footage, photographs, and my memories.

As the teacher of Capoeira, my goals were constantly refined to figure out what was working and to uncover areas that required improvement. Action research requires a systematic way of examining the teaching and learning processes with the goal of determining means of improvement (Benton, 2005; Erickson, 1984; Mertler, 2009; Mills, 2007). Methodologies consistent with action research require data collection, analysis, and implementation (McMillan & Schumacher, 2010; Nolen & Putten, 2007; Riley & Reason, 2015). In alignment with action research and teaching youth in an after-school environment, I examined my data as a tool to sharpen my abilities to explain history, instruct music, and demonstrate physical movements. Building from this framework, I saw each session of the after-school sessions as an opportunity to adjust how I taught the youth of Marcus Chavez Elementary.

## Making Contact

My professional relationship with the research site began when I was hired as the school's physical education teacher. For five years, I was responsible for teaching Capoeira in gym class aligned with the Illinois Physical Education standards and to add to the school's efforts of encouraging social awareness. When I left my teaching position to finish graduate school, I remained involved in the school through identifying other Capoeira teachers to replace me, occasionally assisting classes, and by offering on-site classes in the evenings and weekends as part of entrepreneurial services. When it came time to create this study, my long standing relationship with the school enabled me to establish credibility as an ethical researcher and to recruit volunteer participation from students, teachers, and administrators.

After meeting with the school principal and gaining approval to conduct the study in the 2015–2016 academic year, we decided it would be best to present a proposal to the parents during the school's orientation meeting at the start of the year. In addition to welcoming the parents, describing the school's culture, explaining the guidelines for school uniforms, reviewing discipline policies, providing information about tuition, and articulating other protocols that accompany attending an independent private school, I was added to the agenda to speak about this study. Each of the parents was provided with a copy of the institutional review board (IRB) approved recruitment script. During my presentation, I read verbatim from the script and then allocated time to respond to questions. I answered a series of questions about confidentiality, the mentorship components, and publishing data from the study. At the end of my presentation, I asked the parents to contact me with other concerns or comments.

When conducting investigations with minors, researchers are required to create and collect consent and assent forms. Consent documents are completed by the parents or legal guardians and grant permission for researchers to work with their children. Assent documents mandate the signature of a young person under the age of 18 to include their responses to interview questions, observations, or other data as part of a report, an article, or a book. In alignment with ethical research, I did not coerce the students, or parents to sign the consent and assent documents.

After reading the IRB approved scripts, I passed out the consent and assent forms to teachers, administrators, parents, and students. Following my presentation during the school orientation, I provided each of the adults with copies of the consent documents to review. They were told to return the form to me by the third week of school if interested in participation. During my first after-school meeting I explained the research to the students with an emphasis that participation in the study was not mandatory.

After several weeks, I received consent and assent forms to begin this study. One teacher who taught a course aimed to encourage awareness and social justice activism returned the consent document and agreed to participate in interviews and observations. An administrator who began working with the school when it only offered kindergarten-third grade classes also completed the paperwork to participate in an interview. A total of seven consent and six assent documents were returned from students and parents. Despite permission from his parent, one student did not return the assent document. After expressing a lack of desire to participate in interviews and observation, despite his parent's permission, I did not encourage him to return the form. Ultimately, two members of the Marcus Chavez Elementary staff and five students completed the necessary documentation and fit the criteria to participate in this study.

The majority of the students who attended Marcus Chavez Elementary during the 2015–2016 academic year were Black and Latinx students. Only a group of African-American students returned the IRB approved paperwork to participate. From this group of Black boys and girls, I collected data consistent with the research methods described in this chapter. All students who signed up for the Capoeira after-school program were allowed to participate in the club, however, I only gathered data on the students who provided me with assent and consent documents. For reasons identified in the previous chapters of this book, I decided to focus on the experiences of Black boys.

## Teaching Capoeira and Engaging Dialogue

A critical component of the research methods included teaching the movements, music, history, philosophies, and rituals of Capoeira. On Monday and Wednesday of each week from 3:30 PM to 5:00 PM, I stayed in the school's cafeteria to teach all students who signed up to participate in the after-school program. The numbers fluctuated between a minimum of five to the maximum amount of twenty. Regardless of how many students were in attendance, I attempted to cover each of Capoeira's elements in the allotted time.

The circle in Capoeira where the exchange of physical movements, music, song, and philosophies meet is called a *roda* (*pronounced ho—da*). To begin class, we started in the roda with a brief open discussion covering a topic consistent with the objectives of the study. I sat in a circle with my legs crossed and the students in the center of the cafeteria's floor. Each student was required to share one positive thing about their day with the group before engaging in the day's topic. Topics ranged from nutritional advice to current events impacting communities of color.

Following our discussion, we began to move. I often started with a set of twenty push-ups and fifteen sit-ups. Students were asked to repeat after me as I counted in Brazilian Portuguese and English. Following this first set of warm-up exercises, I often asked students about what they had for lunch. I offered some nutritional feedback and then asked them to continue with another set of exercises selected to get their bodies warm. This cycle of mental dialogue and physical movement assisted the formation of relationships that were necessary for other aspects of the research.

# Observations

To document pedagogical practices and student behaviors, the graduate student who assisted this study and I observed the five students in their academic classes, lunch, and snack periods in the cafeteria and during the after-school Capoeira program. As stated in the previous section, the Capoeira classes were held twice a week. The after-school program ran until about 4:20 PM right before the afternoon snack was provided to all students in the cafeteria. While students, teachers, and after-school facilitators filed into the cafeteria for a snack, I sat and wrote notes from the day's observations.

On the afternoons when the Capoeira program met, we also made a consistent effort to collect field notes during the day regarding the participants' activity in their academic courses that included math, science, social justice, and English. The observation goal was to identify how a culturally responsive curriculum was intertwined in multiple subjects, to see how participants responded to their teachers' instructions, and interacted with their peers. Some of our field note data were documented in real-time as teaching occurred and others were postponed for reflection at the end of the school day.

There were a total of four approaches used to collect observation data of the after-school program that I led as the facilitator and researcher. To capture moments for later reflection, I used a video camera to record ten-minute segments of how I organized the classes and taught Capoeira. Secondarily, I took time after each class to write field notes of my observations on a form I created to briefly capture my experiences. The graduate student who worked with me also took notes once per week while sitting in a corner of the cafeteria so as not to interfere with instruction. In addition to teaching, using a video camera, and collecting field notes, I also used a journal.

My teaching journal served as space where I dumped my ideas and reflections without regards for grammar or punctuation onto paper. Entries reflected my raw experiences in the program and examined the inner dialogue that took place in my head to make sense of Capoeira and the students' response. There were many occasions when I was frustrated by the students' behaviors and other days when I felt the stars aligned perfectly to shine through the young people in class. Each journal entry included the time and date. On average, I wrote one page of open thoughts each day on my experiences as the facilitator of the after-school program.

## Qualitative Interviews

A goal of this research was to capture the voices of students, teachers, and administrators through qualitative interviews. As stated before, I had a professional relationship with the school that began when I worked there as the gym teacher. To minimize biases in responses from my subjects, I solicited the help of a graduate student who collected interview data. Together, we divided the interview tasks to capture the experiences of five students, one teacher, and an administrator. All interviews were recorded, transcribed, and secured to explore how Capoeira influenced the school culture, encouraged academic achievement, and complemented Marcus Chavez Elementary school's social justice mission.

The approaches to conducting interviews with the study's participants differed between groups. Students were interviewed in focus groups and as individuals to understand more about their school experiences and understandings of Capoeira. The graduate student and I questioned the youth participants during their lunch periods and after school. The teacher and administrator were interviewed separately during prearranged appointments within the school day. All interviews took place on the Marcus Chavez Elementary school campus in either the cafeteria, an empty classroom, or an office during times when distractions were minimal.

A semi-structured set of questions was created to learn of the students' and staffs' experiences at Marcus Chavez Elementary **(See Appendices A1–A3)**. There were seven identified questions for the individual interviews and thirteen total that were asked as part of the focus group interview sessions with the students. Interviews with the teachers and administrators included nine questions covering the history of the school, curriculum, and Capoeira. The interviews were designed to take approximately 30–45 minutes to complete.

Interviews were transcribed in alignment with critical race methods and intersectionality theory. With intention, I listened for language consistent with race, age, gender, and the unique voices of people of color. Due to the racial segregation that is common in many Chicago neighborhoods, I was able to see patterns of racism when they talked about their home environments. For example, when students discussed not feeling safe enough to play outside in their communities, I was able to extract an analysis that considered the limited structural resources positioned to influence violence. This intentional approach to transcription empowered me to identify themes in the data to explore this study's hypothesis.

## Teaching Artifacts

To further an understanding of how culturally responsive curriculum and Capoeira influenced the students and Marcus Chavez Elementary school's culture, I kept artifacts from my earliest teaching experiences. This study focused on the after-school program that offered Capoeira as a tool to encourage healthier lifestyles and social awareness, however it was an extension of the physical education program I initiated while in graduate school. I retained examples of the homework assignments, lesson plans, and tests I administered as the physical education teacher to illustrate the foundation for the after-school program **(See Appendices A4–A10)**. Three out of the five student participants in this study also attended Marcus Chavez Elementary when I served as the school's gym teacher.

Student drawings, marketing literature, and class handouts were also collected to gain helpful analysis in the students' experiences at Marcus Chavez Elementary. On multiple occasions, I received pictures drawn by participants in the after-school program that reflected their perceptions of Capoeira and of me as their instructor. We also stored brochures of the school to assess how it marketed itself to recruit additional families. Worksheets provided to students during classroom observations were kept for analysis in how the curriculum aligned with activities assigned in and outside the school. Gathering teaching artifacts helped provide tangible assessment tools to explore the depths of the student, educator, and administrator experiences.

Teaching artifacts also enabled analysis of how the parents of students supported Capoeira. When I worked as the physical education teacher at Marcus Chavez Elementary, I assigned students homework that required parents to observe their children exercising at home. The assignment included routines that reflected the Capoeira movements we trained in class alongside more common bodyweight exercises such as pushups and abdominal crunches **(See Appendix A7)**. Parents were required to sign the worksheet as evidence that the students completed the homework. Dating back to 2010, I retained and secured a total of 416 samples of these training homework assignments with parent signatures. These records, that included notes from parents who indicated they joined their child in the exercises, enabled me to see the value of providing students with work that can encourage healthy activities among families.

## Handling Confidentiality

In collecting interview, observation, teaching artifacts, and other data, it was important to secure the research. All participants were informed of the risks involved in agreeing to serve as subjects in the study through the consent forms and at the beginning of each interview. As the principal investigator, I maintained field notes, photos, and video via a password protected laptop and an external hard drive. While working at the University of Illinois at Chicago, I also kept a locked filing cabinet that stored hard copies of permission documents, field notes, and teaching artifacts.

Students and faculty were asked to keep the discussions of our recorded interviews private. In the student focus groups, I asked everyone to keep the questions and responses inside the dedicated space and time for our conversations. I informed both groups that I would not reveal their identity to teachers or administrators. My goal as the researcher was to extract honest data without fear of repercussion in the event their responses were not positive about some component of the school. Throughout the text pseudonyms are used for the school, students, teachers, and administrators to uphold our confidentiality agreements.

## Epistemological Conclusions

Creating the study to understand more about Capoeira, the school and the African-American male students enrolled at Marcus Chavez Elementary, served as an opportunity to take my interests from the community to the university. The courses I taught to undergraduate students enrolled in the Honors College at the University of Illinois at Chicago grappled with the contemporary implications of social inequalities and borrowed from critical race theory and the history of Capoeira to inform lectures and discussions. From the readings, discussions, and analyses in my courses, I discovered methods that corresponded with documenting the experiences of Black males in educational settings.

This qualitative study included methods consistent with critical race, intersectionality, auto-ethnography, and action research to reveal teaching and learning experiences of Black males enrolled in a K-8 school. Through journaling, collecting observations, conducting interviews with students and staff, and retaining artifacts, I gained an insight into the teaching and learning practices at Marcus Chavez Elementary. By grounding my methods in critical race and intersectionality, I discovered how some students who identified as Black, male, young, and from underserved communities are taught and develop the skills to learn in school. To accurately document the experiences of Black boys, researchers should pursue approaches consistent with the identified methodologies of this chapter and other strategies consistent with capturing authentic insights into their participants' lives.

# References

Benton, J. (2005). *Using action research to foster positive social values*. Lanham, MD: Scarecrow Education.

Bradley, A. M. A. (2009, March 10). *Educational rights of homeless youth: Exploring racial dimensions of homeless educational policy*. Dissertation submitted to the University of Illinois, Chicago.

Brown, T. M., & Rodriguez, L. F. (2009). From voice to agency: Guiding principles for participatory action research with youth. *New Directions for Youth Development, 2009*(123), 19–34.

Camangian, P. (2010). Starting with self: Teaching autoethnography to foster critically caring literacies. *Research in the Teaching of English, 45*(2), 179–204.

Cammarota, J., & Fine, M. (Eds.). (2008). *Revolutionizing education: Youth participatory action research in motion*. New York, NY: Routledge.

Duncan, G. A. (2002). Critical race theory and method: Rendering race in urban ethnographic research. *Qualitative Inquiry, 8*(1), 85–104.

Duncan, G. A. (2005). Critical race ethnography in education: Narrative, inequality and the problem of epistemology. *Race Ethnicity and Education, 8*(1), 93–114

Ellis, C., Adams, T. E., & Bochner, A. P. (2010). Autoethnography: An Overview. *Forum: Qualitative Social Research, 12*(1). Retrieved from http://nbn-resolving.de/urn:nbn:de:0114-fqs1101108

Erickson, F. (1984). What makes school ethnography "ethnographic"? *Anthropology and Education Quarterly, 15*, 51–66.

Gatson, N. S. (2011). The methods, politics, and ethics of representation in online ethnography. In N. K. Denzin & S. L. Yvonna (Eds.), *The Sage handbook of qualitative research* (pp. 513–528). Thousand Oaks, CA: Sage Publications.

Goodall, H. L. (2006). *A need to know: The clandestine history of a CIA family*. Walnut Creek, CA: Left Coast Press.

Hamilton, M. L., Smith, L., & Worthington, K. (2008). Fitting the methodology with the research: An exploration of narrative, self-study and auto-ethnography. *Studying Teacher Education, 4*(1), 17–28.

Harper, S. R. (2009). Niggers no more: A critical race counternarrative on Black male student achievement at predominantly White colleges and universities. *International Journal of Qualitative Studies in Education, 22*(6), 697–712.

Howard, T. C. (2008). Who really cares? The disenfranchisement of African American males in preK-12 schools: A critical race theory perspective. *Teachers College Record, 110*(5), 954–985.

McMillan, J. H., & Schumacher, S. (2010). *Research in education: Evidence-based inquiry, MyEducationLab Series*. Hoboken, NJ: Pearson Education.

Mertler, C. A. (2009). *Action research teachers as researchers in the classroom* (2nd ed.). Thousand Oaks, CA: Sage.

Mills, G. E. (2007). *Action research: A guide for the teacher researcher* (3rd ed.). Upper Saddle River, NJ: Merrill/Prentice Hall.

Neumann, M. (1999). *On the rim: Looking for the Grand Canyon*. Minneapolis, MN: University of Minnesota Press.

Nolen, A. L., & Putten, J. V. (2007). Action research in education: Addressing gaps in ethical principles and practices. *Educational Researcher, 36*(7), 401–407.

Riley, S., & Reason, P. (2015). Cooperative inquiry: An action research practice. In A. J. Smith (Ed.), *Qualitative psychology: A practical guide to research methods* (pp. 168–198). Thousand Oaks, CA: Sage Publications.

Rodriguez-Valls, F. (2016). Pedagogy of the immigrant: A journey towards inclusive classrooms. *Teachers and curriculum, 16*(1), 41–48.

Romero, F. A., & Cammarota, J. (2009). A social justice epistemology and pedagogy for Latina/o students: Transforming public education with participatory action research. *New Directions for Youth Development, 2009*(123), 53–65.

Solórzano, G. D., & Yosso, J. T. (2016). Critical race methodology counter-storytelling as an analytical framework for educational research. In E. Taylor, D. Gillborn, & G. Ladson-Billings (Eds.), *Foundations of critical race theory in education* (pp. 131–141). New York, NY: Routledge.

Stovall, D. (2006). From hunger strike to high school: Youth development, social justice and school formation. In S. A. Ginwright, P. Noguera, & J. Cammarota (Eds.), *Beyond resistance! Youth activism and community change: New democratic possibilities for practice and policy for America's youth* (pp. 97–109). New York, NY: Routledge.

Tate, IV, W. F. (1997). Critical race theory and education: History, theory, and implications. *Review of research in education, 22*(1), 195–247.

Thomas, S. (2010). Ethnography. In G. Mey & K. Mruck (Eds.), *Handbook on qualitative research in psychology* (pp. 462–475). Wiesbaden: Verlag/Springer.

## · 3 ·

# FROM GYM CLASS TO
# THE COMMUNITY

At the start of the 2015–2016 academic year, I had nine years of experience in Capoeira. As discussed in the introduction and preface to this book, I began my journey learning from a student of Mestra Marisa. Years later, I began working with Mestre Calango, a master Capoeira teacher born in Brazil and a member of the United Capoeira Association. Headquartered in Berkeley, California, United Capoeira Association (UCA), was founded by Mestre Acordeon, Mestre Rá, and Mestra Suelly. The founders alongside my teacher, Mestre Calango were integral in my development as a Capoeirista. They encouraged me to explore new depths of physical movements, musical skills, my ideas, and the research of Capoeira in the African continent and in Brazil. In this chapter, I share many of my first experiences as a Capoeira teacher. I illustrate how my approaches to engaging students in critical dialogue evolved and led to my roles as a business owner, volunteer after-school facilitator, and researcher for this study.

The historical lessons and approaches to movement, music, philosophies, and rituals I learned under the tutelage of the United Capoeira Association are what I shared with students enrolled in the after-school program at Marcus Chavez Elementary. As a student, I learned that the seeds of Capoeira were born in Africa and they blossomed in resistance to slavery in Brazil.

Through attending events, taking classes, and reading Mestre Acordeon's book (Almeida, 1986), I was taught about the legacy of Mestre Bimba and other pioneers in Capoeira.

Private conversations I shared with Mestre Acordeon about Mestre Bimba and the purpose of the roda influenced my approaches to class. Mestre Acordeon said that Mestre Bimba, similar to other teachers, did not often use the roda to discuss critical social justice issues. Bimba primarily used the roda to teach Capoeira and secondarily to discuss the folklore, philosophies, and other figures who contributed to the community. In my interpretation of Bimba's work and other great Mestres aligned with his lineage, I implemented another vision for the roda.

I was influenced by the dominant oral histories of Capoeira. These narratives include three similar hypotheses: (1) Capoeira began as a dance in Angola as part of a rites of passage ritual; (2) Capoeira started in Brazil and despite the self-defense elements it was never used to engage combat with the Portuguese; and (3) Capoeira was born through the creativity of African people from multiple nations and involuntarily transported to Brazil where it became a martial art resource for combat, and a tool for cultural retention to resist Portuguese oppression. Teachers and students often engage in debates about which of these origins of Capoeira is correct during classes and annual promotion ceremonies called *Batizados*. When I began teaching, I felt compelled to pass speculations and facts about Capoeira's history to my students.

## An Open House Opened Minds

My first experiences at Marcus Chavez Elementary started before the 2009–2010 academic year. The owners invited me and my then-fiancée to attend an open house for the school. During our time at the open house, I was impressed with the school's mission, its facilities in the city's center, and the staff. As my fiancée was under consideration for a third-grade teaching position, I began to float around the idea of proposing a position for myself as the physical education teacher. Before we left the open house, I briefly talked to one of the owners about teaching Capoeira to the students as the school's physical education instructor.

In 2009, I had three years of experience in Capoeira that included a trip to Brazil. I witnessed the benefits that accompanied training Capoeira. Before joining the United Capoeira Association, I did not have the endorsement from a formal academy to teach students. Nonetheless, I followed-up with the owner who seemed excited about the idea of having a gym teacher who taught Capoeira. We scheduled an interview where I explained my passion for Capoeira and described the health benefits that included cardio and strength building exercises. They accepted my proposal, I was hired and made responsible for building a curriculum that upheld the Illinois Physical Education standards and the unique history, self-defense, acrobatics, dance, philosophies, and rituals of Capoeira.

During the employment orientation for Marcus Chavez Elementary, I learned a lot about the history of the school. I was told it began as an early-learning daycare facility located in a lower-income community that served primarily families of color. Marcus Chavez Elementary started in response to a community meeting where parents expressed concerns about local public education options. Marcus Chavez Elementary school's owners were parents themselves and wanted to have an opportunity to shape the education of their children. Following the community meeting, they began to plan an extension of the early learning services, which over time, led to a school.

Marcus Chavez Elementary started with a kindergarten class and added an additional year with the completion of each successful academic term. Owners of Marcus Chavez began the school with the intention to create a culturally responsive curriculum that considered students' racial, ethnic, economical, and other identities. When I began to teach Capoeira as the physical education teacher, the intent to use activities and curriculum reflective of the students' backgrounds was extended to include gym class.

From the day the school transitioned from an early-learning facility, to the moment kindergarten classes were offered, many of the students who attended Marcus Chavez Elementary were Black or Latinx. The student demographics reflected the location of the daycare's community that had limited quality public school options. Offering an education to students from underserved backgrounds was central to the school's mission of providing an excellent education while also transforming young people into social and political agents for change (Lindsay, 2018b).

## Capoeira as Physical Education Class

Through having the opportunity to share Capoeira as part of a culturally responsive physical education course, I saw myself as an extension of my ancestors via the African diaspora. The Capoeira Master, Manoel dos Reis Machado, otherwise known as Mestre Bimba, is regarded as a pioneer, because he developed a physical education curriculum and opened the first formal academy for Capoeira in Salvador, Bahia, Brazil (Almeida, 1986; Capoeira, 2002; Essien, 2008; Lewis, 1992). Although Bimba has been criticized for his decisions to use self-defense movements from other martial art traditions and his choice to teach primarily wealthier citizens, his role was pivotal in the expansion of Capoeira (Assunção, 2005; Downey, 2005; Talmon-Chvaicer, 2008). As the physical education teacher at Marcus Chavez Elementary, I had the opportunity to add to the legacy of others similar to Mestre Bimba. Not by any measure, could I call myself a Capoeira master, but I was responsible for inspiring cultural retention, healthier lifestyle choices, and social awareness via Capoeira.

In Capoeira, the *roda*, or circle, is where practitioners use percussion instruments and songs to guide two individuals in their exchange of attack and defense sequences. The *berimbau*, often described as a musical bow, is an instrument resembling a bow and arrow, played by using a wooden stick to strike a metal wire while moving a stone back and forth. An *atabaque* is a large wooden hand drum standing 3–5 feet; it is often secured with metal rings and wooden wedges. A *pandeiro* is a tambourine made of goatskin, wood, and metal jingles. An *agogô* often consists of two metal bells and is played when struck by a wooden stick. The *reco-reco* is a piece of bamboo wood, cut in a cylindrical shape with ridges that are scrapped in rhythm with the other musical instruments. With the berimbau as the lead instrument that commands the tone and pace of the others, these percussion instruments guide the tempo of the music in the roda. The songs sung by the roda's participants, coupled with the instruments, determine the *axé* or invisible energy of the roda.

In addition to using the roda for the practice of music and movement, I also used it as a circle for instruction and dialogue. The roda served as the starting and ending points of the classes. It was where I explained self-defense tactics, history, philosophies, and music. The roda also became an established space for meaningful and intimate discussions with students about their environment, identities, injustices, and influences. In my first gym classes, my interpretation of the roda and the appropriate language to explain race and history was met with mixed results.

## Learning by Failing

The space to teach Capoeira at Marcus Chavez Elementary was located in a designated area called the Gross Motor room. It was an open space lined with floor to ceiling windows, a carpeted floor, and four water fountains. The Gross

Motor room was located near the students' bathrooms and the first, second, and third-grade classrooms. The room offered great natural light, but its location near the restrooms and the entrances to three classrooms, was often counterproductive to encouraging students to give me their undivided attention.

In September of 2009, I taught my first classes in Capoeira. My first groups of students were in kindergarten through third grade. Each class came to me with strengths and weakness. I learned very soon that there was not a one-size-fits-all approach to effectively engage students, ranging in age from 5–9, in a physical activity. It was challenging to explain how the social construct of race led to the racism that inspired enslaved Africans to resist through Capoeira.

Before teaching my first class, another educator informed me of how important it was to establish authority quickly when working with young people. Per the advice I received, I prepared myself by creating a set of rules for the Gross Motor room. I decided to recite the rules at the start of each class to reaffirm my role as teacher and my students' responsibilities to demonstrate respect toward me and their peers. Although I had a plan, my first class taught me that a strict, no-nonsense approach interfered with my objectives to build community and to introduce the young people to the purposes of the class.

Before the first group of students arrived, I took the time to prepare the space. My preparation included clearing the Gross Motor room from debris and other school items, placing the instruments out for display, and warming my body up with some calisthenics exercises. I moved as quickly as possible to create an environment for Capoeira while also preparing my body and mind for the students. It took longer than I expected. My first class nearly ambushed me as I sat on the floor stretching with my back in the opposite direction of their entrance into the Gross Motor room.

I didn't see the third-grade class arrive. They interfered with my plans that included greeting them with a standing power pose. Quickly, I made the adjustment to sit on the floor with my chest wide and hands balled into fists while resting on my waist similar to the iconic Superman image. This pose was my attempt to create body language that reflected confidence, power, and a spirit of courage that Cuddy (2015) states is critical when facing fears. I was concerned about how to introduce myself, make a positive first impression, and establish the image that a seasoned teacher told me was essential to successful classroom management.

After a series of awkward looks and snide remarks by the students in response to my sitting Superman pose I began my first class as *Instrutor* Lindsay. I told the students, Brazilian Portuguese is the language spoken in Brazil where

Capoeira developed as a response to slavery and that the word, "instrutor," translates to "instructor" in English. My first attempt to engage the students began with the question, "What is Capoeira?" Many of them had never heard the word Capoeira, before that day. I responded, "Capoeira is an art form created by enslaved Africans that combines acrobatics, music, dance, and self-defense" (Lindsay, 2018b). From left to right, I saw the smiles on the students' faces transfer from one mouth to the next after I offered this definition.

The looks of excitement and curiosity changed when I asked them to join hands and make a circle in the center of the room. I wanted to explain more about the history of Capoeira, and the significance of the roda in class. My comments began with, "The circle in Capoeira is called a roda and it is where Capoeiristas move in rhythm to the musical instruments" (Lindsay, 2018b). The students responded with facial expressions that I interpreted as confusion and convinced me to provide a more detailed definition.

I explained that the literal translation of the word roda is wheel in English. It is the space wherever Capoeira is trained in formal academies and in streets. The roda is where the conversation happens. The conversation of Capoeira is an exchange of kicks, evasive movements, philosophies, rituals, and acrobatics to the rhythm of percussion instruments. Capoeira instruments are placed at the entrance to the roda. They command the attention of people who sing and clap for the two Capoeristas engaged in the *jogo* or game. I continued with my best descriptions of the roda and Capoeira until it was time to discuss race.

One of my journal entries illustrates an effort to have a meaningful conversation, real talk, about race and Capoeira with my first class. As this example shows, I encountered challenges in my role as the physical education and Capoeira teacher to implement the roda as space for critical dialogue with my students.

> September 8, 2009                                        8:00 PM
>
> Today, I taught my first class and tried to explain race. I should've thought about using different language because when I gave them an academic definition from my CRT [critical race theory] class, they looked at me as if I was crazy. I thought that I was explaining the concept clearly and direct but the responses I received told me a different story. They gave me a confused look and appeared to silently say, "huh?" I should have expected this response, but how was I supposed to know they would respond that way. I am brand new to teaching this age group, and I have a lot to learn. (Lindsay, 2018b)

This entry from my teaching journal identifies how my desire to use the roda for candid conversation did not align with the students, because I spoke with academic jargon, instead of using age-appropriate vocabulary. Consistent with action research, this paragraph of my journal also reflects the impetus to improve as a communicator to young people. With this passage, is also possible to observe how engaging students of color with candid race discussions did not occur overnight. The most important takeaway from this quote is that although we can recognize race and racism as central in our everyday lives, talking about it is not often taught in school and especially with young children.

Through a series of successes and failures, I learned that conversations about race and racism in physical education classes with young people requires an intentional pedagogical strategy. For example, it is often better to ask a direct question about a student's environment, rather than to use academic jargon to explain the implications of racism before proceeding to have dialogue. Such an example of phrasing might include language such as, "how is the block you live on," contrary to, "how does racism impact the level of violence that permeates your community" (Lindsay, 2018b). With the phrasing, "how is the block you live on," my students shared that while they liked their neighborhoods, they often did not feel safe playing outside. They discussed individual behaviors, organizations, and underground economies, products of systemic racism, that included gangs, violence, and drugs.

When I started to teach Capoeira, I was also a graduate student enrolled in a critical race theory course that shaped my thoughts and the language to discuss social inequalities. I had a difficult time explaining the significance of racism to young people because I spent a significant amount of time in conversations with adults. To be effective in my role as a physical education teacher with a social justice mindset, I needed to translate graduate school-level terminology into language digestible for a five-year-old child.

## Kindergarten Students Do Not Sit Still

One of my most challenging groups to teach at Marcus Chavez Elementary included the kindergarten classes. On the first day, they showed me the imperativeness of explaining Capoeira quick, precise, and void of the word, "gymnastics."

September 10, 2009                                                    6:00 PM
Kindergarten has been by far the most difficult of all my classes. They had so much energy and did not want to sit down. I talked with my first group for ten minutes about how capoeira began among enslaved Africans in Brazil. I mentioned that it incorporates self-defense with music and flips like some may have seen in gymnastics.

> As soon as I said the word gymnastics, and before I could complete another sentence, one student yelled "wee" and began to do cartwheels! The other students laughed and soon after followed suit. I'm exhausted. (Lindsay, 2018b)

Reflective of culturally responsive theories and practices, I explained Capoeira in language suitable to my students' background. They knew the word gymnastics and responded. Although it was not the response I hoped for, as, it interrupted my lesson plan, it however confirmed that the vocabulary I used did correspond with their identities. In this quote from my teaching journal, it is possible to observe how I defined Capoeira for young people with the history of slavery at the center. It's also clear to see how I failed to capture the young people's attention span in the opening moments of a gym class where they anticipated ample opportunities to run, jump, and scream.

Throughout my first year of teaching Capoeira to young people, I learned about my strengths and weaknesses as a teacher. Many students enjoyed gym because I structured acrobatic games alongside Capoeira instruction in nearly every class. Despite my best attempts at brevity, some students believed I over-explained movements, music, or the roots of Capoeira. Kindergarten classes were especially difficult for me because many of the students did not want anything to do with sitting during a class they perceived empowered them to move without the restriction of their classroom desks.

While teaching at Marcus Chavez Elementary, I experienced some triumphs and even more challenges. On one occasion, I looked to one of my coworkers for encouragement but instead was discouraged when he belittled physical education professionals.

> September 11, 2009                                              6:30 PM
> I talked to Frank today about my first week. I was hoping to get advice, but this bastard offered criticism. He listened to my account of yesterday and frustrations with explaining race to my classes. I also told him about how difficult it was to engage kindergartners in an hour of organized physical activity. His response was, "those who can teach, teach, and those that cannot teach, teach gym." He said it was just a saying, but I believe he meant PE teachers are less competent than other teachers. It was offensive because it inferred that I was not a teacher due to my early struggles in the classroom. He pissed me off. (Lindsay, 2018b)

I was angry after my conversation with Frank. I intended to gain some insights to improvement from a seasoned teacher, but he only offered comments that made me more upset about some of my first classes. It was clear to me that he did not perceive physical education as an important subject, or respect the

teachers who decided to specialize in this area. Frank's attitude was reflective of the growing trend that schools take to eliminate the gym period in
exchange for more time in science, technology, engineering, and mathematics
(STEM) courses.

Despite my frustration with Frank and the negative perception of physical
education he conveyed to me, I began to explore new methods to improve my
gym classes. Through examining the Illinois Physical Education Standards,
reflecting on my teaching experiences, and thinking about Capoeira's history, I created lesson plans that began with movement, incorporated history,
and allowed time for discussions. For example, while I demonstrated the base
stance for Capoeira called *Ginga*, I simultaneously talked about the history of
Capoeira and other topics that I discovered were relevant to the lives of the
students. I translated Brazilian Portuguese terms into English, so my students
could understand the messages of the songs, dance movements, self-defense
kicks, acrobatics, and rituals.

## Creating Roda Real Talk

Over time with small adjustments, I established dedicated time near the beginning and end of classes to talk in the roda. When we had conversations, I
made it a top priority to use language that reflected my students' backgrounds.
I asked questions such as, "what block do you live on?; What did you have for
lunch?; and, What's something you like to change in your neighborhood?"
In alignment with critical race theory, their responses served as counterstories to dominant narratives that claim all young people have access to equal
resources (Yosso, 2006). These opportunities for unfiltered dialogue enabled
me to learn more about my students and to offer health and fitness related
advice. Our conversations served as a gateway to discuss race and to foster
opportunities to create the relationships necessary to connect with students
and to improve as a teacher.

In addition to using a journal to document my class observations and
improvement strategies, I also began to use a video camera to record classes. In
alignment with action research and auto-ethnography, the camera offered me
an additional resource to review my teaching practices. In addition to clarify-
ing some of the observations documented in my teaching journals, the camera
helped me to reorganize lesson plans and, as a bonus, it served as a valuable
tool to assist with classroom management. When students decided Capoeira
was too hard, and they would rather play with friends, I used the presence of

the camera to remind them that I had video footage of their shenanigans! Just the idea that I had evidence to show their parents, classroom teachers, or the principal was often enough to correct misbehavior.

The camera helped me to identify the benefits and drawbacks of the teaching strategies, I attempted to establish with each class. I started every class the same way with students lining up on the white wall of the Gross Motor room. Next, we reviewed the rules and clarified my expectations for the period. Whenever new students transferred to the school, I introduced Capoeira as a martial art and asked my current students to help with explaining the history and other elements that make it unique and valuable to practice at Marcus Chavez Elementary. The benefit of having a routine to begin each class fostered a collective understanding of the expectations for Capoeira class. To gain a few laughs from their peers, some decided to resist waiting for class and instead decided to run around the Gross Motor room while others lined up along the white wall.

The first fifteen minutes of each class was critical to the success of the period. It is during these initial moments, that I often said, "*faz uma roda*" (Make a wheel/circle), where we would begin our warm-up exercises and clarify the day's learning objectives. Analyzing the video footage captured of these early class moments empowered me to understand how beginning with a group activity was critical to establishing an expectation for engagement. The structure of the circle allowed students to look around and see each other as active participants in Capoeira. They praised each other when they succeeded in copying my movements or playing the instruments. They were also quick to tease when someone made a mistake.

In the video footage captured, I saw the potential of the roda to teach Capoeira, encourage healthy habits, and to discuss topics relevant to the lives of the students. I often asked the young people about their communities, school lunches, and experiences in other classes. Questions as mentioned above, "how is the block you live on," and, "What did you have for lunch?" proved instrumental in creating meaningful dialogue, real talk, with the students. We talked about race when they told me where they lived and the importance of making healthy food choices when they shared about their lunch meals. My goal was to make consistent time in class to talk about Capoeira, exercise, and topics relevant to the students' experiences.

The camera revealed my triumphs and failures to create real talk in a school environment that welcomed social justice as a component of every class, including physical education. The students were accustomed to courses at Marcus Chavez Elementary where teachers tried to create lesson plans that reflected students' racial, gender, ethnic, and other identities. Administrators told me explicitly to ensure the young people knew the roots of Capoeira and how it began among enslaved Africans as a resistance tool against European colonialism. Through my attempts to engage conversations about communities of color, racial oppression, and the origins of Capoeira, I hoped to fulfill my responsibilities as an employee and as someone dedicated to upholding the teachings of critical race theory (Artiles, 2016) and culturally responsive pedagogy (Ladson-Billings, 2009).

Aligned with acknowledging the systemic nature of racism influences people of color's perception of themselves, I encouraged my students to embrace positive self-awareness and believe they possess the ability to do well in school. I often found a need to remind my students of their potential, affirmed by the accomplishments of people of color in the past. Whenever they failed to complete the push-up or sit-up set assigned, I made comments such as, "remember your ancestors," and, "be mindful of the people who created Capoeira. They didn't give up and neither can you." My expectations did not demand that students would execute every Capoeira movement or play an instrument perfect every single time, but I did require that they try to do their best.

Another critical observation of the video was my consistency in remembering to translate Brazilian Portuguese terms used in the Capoeira community into English. The primary language of many of my students was English. Culturally responsive curriculum requires using the students' dominant language in all instruction. When students looked at me and did not respond to my instructions, it was often a result of me explaining something in Portuguese and not in English. Demonstration became the universal language all students understood when it was difficult for me to adequately translate concepts unique to the practice of Capoeira.

## Homework and Student Drawings as Evidence

One of the initiatives that made Capoeira class unique at Marcus Chavez Elementary was the homework [see Figure 3.1] assignments provided to students. I asked students to train the exercises covered in class at home with the supervision of an adult or another responsible young person. I intended to instill the idea of exercise as a lifestyle decision, not limited to gym class.

Name:
Date: 11/ 10 , 2010
Grade: 2

Instructor Lindsay

Capoeira training week of Jan 10

**Directions: Do these Capoeira exercises with the supervision of your parent/guardian or designated adult. These exercises should be done at least two days per week. Be sure to drink water as needed in between exercises (6-8 ounces every 15 minutes). This signed assignment is due every MONDAY at the start of class.**

**Exercises should be completed in this order:**

1. **2 sets of 15 pushups**

2. **2 sets of 15 sit ups**

3. **Ginga** for **5** minutes without stopping (remember to protect your face and keep a low stance)

4. Warm up **stretch**

5. **10 Sequencia Um (sequence 1)- 1. Esquiva latera; 2. Mao atras (place hand behind; 3. Negativa; 4. Role (Oh-lay); 5. Esquiva Latera 6. Check 7. Ginga**

6. **Stretch** all major muscle groups

**Please circle two days that these exercises were completed:**

Sunday  (Monday)  Tuesday      (Wednesday)    Thursday      Friday      Saturday

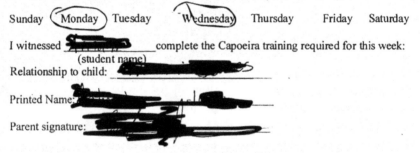

I witnessed ▓▓▓▓▓ complete the Capoeira training required for this week:
       (student name)
Relationship to child: ▓▓▓▓▓

Printed Name: ▓▓▓▓▓

Parent signature: ▓▓▓▓▓

Figure 3.1: Anonymous Student Homework Sample.
Source: Author

As parents wrote me notes and students drew pictures on the back of the assignments, they also became an additional source of student feedback. In May of 2010, I wrote the following entry in my teaching journal:

May 3, 2010                                                               6:00 PM

Today, I was reinforced by Josh that the work I am doing with Capoeira is making a difference. He returned his homework and told me that he loves Capoeira. He said that he completed the homework and the exercises with his dad! He went on to say how he didn't feel safe playing outside, because of the violence in his community. While I am happy that he practiced Capoeira outside of class, I feel that my work may be in vain if I can't figure out a way to address systemic racism and impact his community on a greater scale. I am happy that he is exercising with his family, but I can't help but feel there is more that needs my attention. Two additional students gave me drawings that they created, depicting me as a Capoeira superhero. It looks nothing like me, except for dreads, but it is an indicator that I must be doing something right. (Lindsay, 2018b)

While I was thrilled with the feedback from my student, Josh, I also felt a sense of inadequacy as revealed in this entry. It was great to know that students were encouraged to exercise with their parents and also disturbing to receive the reminder that violence was plaguing their communities. From this passage in my journal, it is possible to see the impact that I made, and the desire I possessed to do more meaningful work. Teaching artifacts in the form of feedback on homework assignments and student illustrations served as evidence that Capoeira has the potential to act a valuable component of culturally responsive physical education curricula.

Figure 3.2 is one of the more memorable drawings I received from a student who was enrolled at Marcus Chavez Elementary during the 2010–2011 academic year. In this picture, there is an original illustration of me along with my student and his younger brothers. I believe he drew me aligned with his vision of my roles as a leader, role model, or father figure. There is also the name of Zumbi, short for Zumbi dos Palmares, who was a legendary Capoeirista who defended a famous *quilombo*, a Maroon community in Brazil, against the Portuguese. Zumbi dos Palmares was one of the figures discussed in class as an example of how resistance was integral to the practice of Capoeira. It's these types of student drawings and other teaching artifacts that empowered me to understand the impact I was making in the lives of young people through Capoeira.

Throughout my time as a teacher at Marcus Chavez Elementary I retained other samples of students' work for assessment and to decide if they were duplicable for future use. Soon after the Capoeira gym classes grew in popularity, I was asked to start an after-school club for students with interests in going deeper into the subject. Any student who wished to participate in the club was required to complete an application consisting of multiple documents.

Figure 3.2: Anonymous Student Drawing.
Source: Author

With the packet, I hoped to identify students who were serious about their training and learning of the concepts presented in the gym class.

The application packet included a letter of recommendation form for the applicant's classroom teacher to complete, a parent survey that asked about their child's leadership behaviors at home and in their community, and a waiver in case of injury. The letter of recommendation was a form letter that enabled teachers to confirm a student met the academic requirements of a "C" or better in all subjects and that they were well-behaved in class. To assess whether the student engaged in leadership activities outside of school, I asked parents to sign a letter that indicated whether their child demonstrated respect at home and picked up litter in the community. The waiver was a standard requirement carried over from the gym class that explained the risks and benefits of that could accompany the training of any martial art. Most students who desired to participate in the Capoeira Club returned the documents before the return date. The excitement that students displayed about Capoeira affirmed the potential for growth beyond the gym class.

## Batizados, Leadership Changes, and Company Beginnings

After taking a memorable trip to Brazil with a group of Marcus Chavez Elementary students, teachers, and administrators at the end of the 2009–2010 academic year, I began to offer classes in the evenings and on the weekends as a sole proprietor. The trip to Brazil was made possible by Marcus Chavez's international study initiative to connect the curriculum studied in the classroom to tactile experiences in the world. Capoeira classes coincided with the school's program that explored Brazil as the focal country during the 2009–2010 term. After witnessing the growth of the Marcus Chavez Elementary students in Brazil via interactions with Brazilian youth in Capoeira classes, I was encouraged by administrators to expand classes to the community.

Two of the administrators who also owned the school provided me with the Gross Motor room in the evenings and on the weekends, free of charge. All Marcus Chavez Elementary school students and their parents who took these additional classes were offered discounted rates. Several took advantage of this opportunity for more instruction, and the classes grew in popularity. I began working with another local Capoeira group to assist in the expansion of the program to other communities. Together, we emphasized the roots of Capoeira and the self-discipline required to train and study for improvement.

In 2011, we organized the first *Batizado*. A Batizado, which translates to baptism in English, is an integral component of Capoeira communities that brings together students and teachers from around the world. Over the course of five days, Batizados provide intense training workshops, lectures, performances, and other relationship building activities. Notable Capoeira masters, Mestre Acordeon, Mestra Suelly, and my teacher Mestre Calango attended and facilitated classes during our first event. The pinnacle moment of this annual event is the Batizado ceremony where new students are inducted into the community, and more experienced students receive promotion through a series of physical and mental tests.

The students at Marcus Chavez Elementary encouraged me to organize the first Batizado. Learning the martial art components of Capoeira, they wanted to receive recognition similar to a Karate student who earns belts after spending time developing their skills. At the Batizado, the students were thrilled to wear the traditional white Capoeira uniform and earn the hand-made belt, cordão, at the end of the weekend. When students returned to school in the 2011–2012 school year, it appeared that wearing the uniform to class encouraged some to intensify their focus in class.

At the end of the 2012 school year, we held our second Batizado with a larger group of children and adults. Several students alongside their parents began to take classes in the evenings and on the weekends. My teacher, Mestre Calango made several visits to the school to teach and to bring supplies. The 2012 school year brought about a significant change in the leadership and structure of Capoeira at Marcus Chavez Elementary.

Throughout the time that I served as the physical education teacher and coordinator at Marcus Chavez Elementary, I was also enrolled in the Ph.D. program in Policy Studies in Urban Education at the University of Illinois at Chicago. Marcus Chavez Elementary school's administrators allowed me to create a schedule that enabled me to attend graduate classes and fulfill my work responsibilities. As I made progress in the graduate program that required more of my time, I became increasingly less available to teach all students. In 2012, as I worked to finish my dissertation, Mestre Calango moved to Chicago and assumed my position as the gym teacher.

When I was not writing chapters or conducting research for my dissertation, I would assist Mestre Calango's gym classes and learn from him to improve my skills and knowledge of Capoeira. Many of the students who began Capoeira with me in 2009 remained enrolled at Marcus Chavez Elementary and continued to grow under the leadership of Mestre Calango. Mestre Calango expanded my teachings of the culture surrounding Capoeira. He helped students learn more complex physical movements, Brazilian Portuguese, and how to make many of the instruments used in class.

In 2013, we organized our third Batizado and decided to form a limited liability company called UCA Chicago, L3c. United Capoeira Association—Chicago, UCA Chicago L3c, derived from the gym classes and after-school club that I co-facilitated with Mestre Calango. With the success of the Batizados and classes at Marcus Chavez, the company demonstrated much potential for growth. Through UCA Chicago, L3c, we expanded classes to other schools in the city and surrounding suburbs.

From 2013–2015, two additional Batizados were held that included students from outside Marcus Chavez Elementary. In this time, Mestre Calango returned to live in Brazil for an extended time but continued to mentor me and provide additional resources. A young adult student of mine was hired to teach the gym classes at Marcus Chavez as I began work as a Postdoctoral Fellow in Teaching and Mentoring with the University of Illinois at Chicago's Honors College. Similar to when Mestre Calango worked as the physical education teacher, I visited Marcus Chavez to assist and lead classes as part of my commitments to Capoeira, the school, community, and success of the program.

In 2015, six years after the first gym classes began with a focal point of Capoeira as a means of instruction at Marcus Chavez Elementary, the research for this study began. Although UCA Chicago L3c existed as a business entity, I volunteered my time as the principal investigator to uncover the impact of Capoeira on students enrolled in the after-school program. As the once gym teacher now serving as a volunteer and after-school facilitator, my goal was to offer services via Capoeira and to understand how a complex art form could serve the interests of young Black males and make a social justice impact in their communities.

## Concluding Thoughts

From 2009 to 2016, I led the Capoeira program at Marcus Chavez Elementary. During this time, ample resources were poured into students to develop their comprehension of Capoeira's movements, philosophies, music, history, and rituals. Throughout my time with Marcus Chavez Elementary, I occupied many roles from full-time teacher to the after-school researcher and volunteer assumed for this study. Each moment was made possible through the legacy transferred to me through the spirits of my ancestors enslaved in the Americas.

As a person of African descent who taught Capoeira to the young people at Marcus Chavez Elementary, I felt compelled to share how race, racism, class, and gender shaped the enslavement of people in Brazil and the United States. I believed it was my responsibility to connect the history to their contemporary experiences. My journal entries, teaching artifacts, and other data indicate I achieved my goals with mixed results. Some students were intrigued by Capoeira and others were only concerned with the opportunity to move beyond the constraints of their classroom desks. As expressed in forthcoming chapters through the voices of my students, and young Black males in particular, I demonstrate how a unique after-school program encouraged awareness and actions aligned with social justice.

# References

Almeida, B. (1986). *Capoeira, a Brazilian art form: History, philosophy, and practice*. Berkeley, CA: North Atlantic Books.

Artiles, J. A. (2016). Toward an interdisciplinary understanding of educational equity and difference. In E. Taylor, D. Gillborn & G. Ladson-Billings (Eds.), *Foundations of critical race theory in education* (pp. 157–180). New York, NY: Routledge.

Assunção, M. R. (2005). *Capoeira: The history of an Afro-Brazilian martial art*. New York, NY: Routledge.

Capoeira, N. (2002). *Capoeira: Roots of the dance-fight-game*. Berkeley, CA: Blue Snake Books.

Cuddy, A. (2015). *Presence: Bringing your boldest self to your biggest challenges*. New York, NY: Little, Brown and Company.

Downey, G. (2005). *Learning capoeira: Lessons in cunning from an Afro-Brazilian art*. New York, NY: Oxford University Press.

Essien, A. (2008). *Capoeira beyond Brazil: From a slave tradition to an international way of life*. Berkeley, CA: Blue Snake Books.

Ladson-Billings, G. (2009). *The dreamkeepers: Successful teachers of African American Children*. San Francisco, CA: Jossey-Bass.

Lewis, L. J. (1992). *Ring of liberation: Deceptive discourse in Brazilian Capoeira*. Chicago, IL: University of Chicago Press.

Lindsay, V. (2018a). *Critical race and education for black males: When pretty boys become men*. New York, NY: Peter Lang.

Lindsay, V. (2018b). Roda real talk: A physical education teacher's effort to use the capoeira circle as a tool to encourage critical dialogue. In E. Mendoza, B. Kirshner, & K. Gutiérrez (Eds.), *Power, equity, and (re)design: Bridging learning and critical theories in learning ecologies for youth* (pp. 77–92). Charlotte, NC: Information Age Press.

Talmon-Chvaicer, M. (2008). *The hidden history of capoeira: A collision of cultures in Brazilian battle dance*. Austin, TX: University of Texas Press.

Yosso, J. T. (2006). *Critical race counterstories along the Chicana/Chicano educational pipeline*. New York, NY: Routledge.

## · 4 ·

# WHEN BLACK MALES SPEAK

Walking into the cafeteria at the Marcus Chavez Elementary school's new location, I could sense the energies of struggle and freedom. On the East green wall were illustrations of notable Black and Latinx historical figures spray painted by a local graffiti artist. The South wall displayed the school's name, mission, and an Adinkra symbol meaning to value culture, history, and progress. In this recently acquired secondary location of Marcus Chavez Elementary, the space that served as the lunchroom also doubled as the after-school space for Capoeira in the afternoons. It was the space between these four walls that enabled the fostering of relationships between myself and young Black males, no older than 10 years old, to learn more about their experiences in their communities.

In 2015, the Marcus Chavez Elementary school operated from two separate buildings in two different communities to serve young people in grades Kindergarten through eighth grade with an additional Gap Year option. The original building where I worked as the gym teacher during graduate school focused on the needs of students enrolled in kindergarten-fourth grade. In the new location, where the research for the after-school program took place, students in grades fifth through the Gap Year were provided with academic classes and extracurricular options. The Gap Year offered students who met the academic requirements of a one grade level above the state standards for eighth grade, an additional year to prepare before attending high school. Each location maintained culturally responsive curricula with an intention to inspire youth toward influencing social justice causes.

As part of the methods indicated in chapter two, my protocol included conducting classroom observations and interviews with student participants. The interviews that followed a semi-structured script and my documented observations provide the data for this chapter. The findings are presented in a narrative format to illustrate the school's secondary location, to provide insight into academic courses and to discuss the after-school program with the voices of this study's five young Black male participants. In the confidentiality interests of the students, all names have been changed. In the tradition of critical race theory methods and research, (Bell, 1987, 1992; Dixson, 2006; Parker & Lynn, 2016; Solórzano & Yosso, 2016; Yosso, 2006), this chapter uses creativity and counter-storytelling as a challenge to majoritarian claims that undermine the unique experiences of people of color.

In this chapter I take you from the entrance of Marcus Chavez Elementary, to the words of my participants. The narrative follows a brief timeline of only four days, but the description of the school, classes, participants, and their experiences shared in the following pages were gathered throughout the 2015–2016 academic year. The dialogue that appears in this text is from the conversations I recorded with five young Black males in small group meetings and during one-on-one interview sessions. Depictions of the school building and classrooms come from field notes collected multiple times each week for nine months. Through this narrative that resembles journal entries, I intend to provide evidence of the value of culturally responsive curriculum, Capoeira, and the potential of young Black males in educational settings to influence school policies and school cultures.

## Monday Capoeira Classes

According to local weather records, (ABC7 Chicago), it was an unseasonably warm November 2, 2015. The high reached 74 degrees Fahrenheit on that first Monday in November when I began to collect data for this study. With my birthday two days away, I accepted the mild weather as a premature gift. After fulfilling my campus duties, I walked for fifteen minutes to the new location of Marcus Chavez Elementary. Despite beginning the Capoeira after-school program in September, it took until November to receive all the

Institutional Review Board approved documents back from students, teachers, and administrators.

The school day started at 7:45 AM and the Capoeira after-school program went from 3:30 PM to 5:00 PM. We didn't spend the whole hour and thirty minutes practicing Capoeira, because, during the last thirty minutes, the school served an afternoon snack for all students in the cafeteria. I arrived at 3:15 PM to set up the instruments for Capoeira class and to prepare the space. I was ready to learn more about the school's culturally responsive curriculum and to begin the assessment of the Capoeira program that I volunteered to lead.

Before the owners began a lease on the building in 2013, the secondary location of Marcus Chavez Elementary was a community center. Although the building was not constructed as a school, it had enough classrooms for all students, alongside dedicated rooms for Spanish language, technology, and science. Unlike the first school building, each of the administrators had separate offices. There was also a fully equipped theater and spacious lunchroom.

When arriving at Marcus Chavez Elementary, it was necessary to enter two sets of glass doors with black frames from the primary parking lot. For security purposes, the first set of doors was often open during the school day; however, the second glass doors required someone from inside the school to manually push open the door or unlock it via a button located near the attendant of the front desk. When I arrived on Monday, November 2, the first set of doors were open while the second doors remained closed. No one was sitting at the front desk and I couldn't see any students or teachers walking around to let me in manually. I had no choice but to wait.

After about five minutes, the school's administrative assistant returned to her desk and opened the door. I walked into an immaculately clean foyer. To my immediate right were two black leather seats with pictures of students hung on the wall above. I could see my reflection in the wooden floors that outlined the school's foyer. Behind the desk sat the administrative assistant dressed in business attire along with a smile across her face.

I said hello and asked her how she was doing, before heading to the cafeteria for Capoeira class. To enter the section of the school building where classes were held, and the cafeteria was located, an additional set of gray doors required a key or the password to enter on an electronic keypad for access. Due to my familiarity with the school, I was trusted with the password to release the lock from the doors. I entered the code, walked approximately ten feet, and turned left to walk inside the cafeteria.

The fluorescent lighting and four large rectangular windows of the cafeteria enabled an abundance of natural light into the space. Brown tiles lined the floor. Besides the two walls painted with the murals, the cafeteria's cement walls were painted white. In between the four large rectangular windows was a United Capoeira Association banner, the Brazilian flag, and Marcus Garvey's red, black, and green Pan-African flag.

The school used foldable and easily transportable tables for lunch periods. All six were down when I arrived for Capoeira class. Instruments, target mitts, kicking bags, and other supplies were locked in a storage room accessible through the cafeteria. The storage room was also the location where I changed from my work clothes to my traditional Capoeira uniform: white pants, white t-shirt, and handmade braided belt of yarn interchangeably called *corda* and *cordão* in Brazilian Portuguese.

By the time I was dressed and had pulled the instruments out from the storage room, it was 3:27 PM. The program was scheduled to begin at any moment, and the tables remained down from the lunch periods. I needed to choose whether to proceed with clearing the space in preparation for the students to arrive or to continue with organizing the Capoeira instruments. Before I could finish rolling one of the tables to a position against the wall, my first student arrived.

## Meeting The Fellas

Jermaine was a fifth-grade student at Marcus Chavez Elementary. From the early days, when I began teaching him Capoeira in kindergarten, he had demonstrated an inclination toward the acrobatic components of the martial art. He often performed an Aú, a cartwheel, whenever he entered the Gross Motor room. When he arrived at the cafeteria on that Monday, I discouraged him from cartwheeling every time he entered the cafeteria, because as a recognized leader among his peers, someone often followed and mimicked, his every move.

At approximately four feet three inches tall, Jermaine was not the tallest student in the program, but his classmates continued to respect his leadership skills. He had a darker brown skin complexion and styled his hair short in an even length. Jermaine's personality was charming and easy going. He frequently had a smile on his face during class and often volunteered to lead exercises for other students.

Soon after Jermaine arrived at Capoeira class on Monday, November 2, 2015, another student, Wesley, came strolling into the cafeteria looking visibly upset. Before Wesley attended Marcus Chavez Elementary, he was labeled a "bad kid." I knew of his history because, similar to Jermaine, he was one of my students when I taught Capoeira at the primary school location. I remember when he transferred to the school in second grade and it was evident that the social-emotional damage that was done in pre-school, kindergarten, and first grade influenced his self-perception and beliefs about appropriate behaviors in schools. Before I could ask him what was wrong, he told me that he got in trouble in class and was concerned about punishment when he made it home.

Wesley had a lighter skin complexion than Jermaine, styled his hair with some length on the top and shorter on the side. This style is often referred to as a fade. He was taller for his age at five feet, five inches with a thin body frame. Unlike Jermaine, Wesley did not possess the same inclination toward acrobatic movements. His body mechanics were awkward and he had a difficult time following the rhythm of the music used in Capoeira. I often found it necessary to remind him to stay focused because he talked frequently during instruction.

Three more students, Steve, Michael, and Jeff walked into the cafeteria together. As soon as they placed one foot in the room, Michael hit Jeff and said, "Tag you're it!" Steve and Michael began to run and scream. With authority in my voice, I called their names and told them to stop playing and to instead assist with moving the tables in preparation for Capoeira class. They slowly acquiesced to my request and began to help Jermaine and Wesley.

Steve was one of my former students from the primary school, but Michael and Jeff were new to Capoeira and to Marcus Chavez Elementary. Michael and Steve were sixth graders, whereas Jeff was in the seventh grade. Steve, approximately five feet two inches with a brown complexion, was strong for his age and could complete thirty push-ups without the need to rest between repetitions. Michael was similar in height to Steve, but he did not appear to have the same amount of physical strength. He could only do fifteen push-ups without rest, but with his Taekwondo background, he was drawn to Capoeira's movements. Jeff was in the seventh grade, five feet six inches tall, fast, and comparable to Jermaine in his ability to execute the acrobatic components of Capoeira.

Jermaine, Wesley, Michael, Steve, and Jeff, "The Fellas," were among the first to arrive to class. Within five minutes sixteen more Black and Brown students walked into the cafeteria to participate in Capoeira. Some came in Capoeira attire and others in their school uniforms. Thanks to The Fellas each of the cafeteria tables were out of the way and against the wall; the space was ready for our session.

I began class the same way as I had for many years. The students were familiar with my requirement that they stand in a quiet line before class starts to wait for instruction. I expected all conversations to stop and although it was a simple request, it proved difficult for young people who spent six hours in academic courses before transitioning to the after-school program. There often were a couple of students who would use the time between their arrival and my instructions to play instead of waiting patiently for class to begin.

My standards were high because I wanted to encourage self-discipline. When I worked as the gym teacher, I overheard another teacher tell students that his goal was to instill the type of discipline that came from within. Meaning that he expected his class to use self-control and not to wait for an adult to correct their behaviors. That teacher's words remained with me, and I expected students to respect the guidelines established during our first and subsequent meetings. I often reminded students that self-discipline is critical to all forms of success including the martial arts.

After five minutes of waiting for all the students to get in line and provide me with their undivided attention, we were ready to begin. I commanded, "Faz uma roda. Make a circle." Those six words in Brazilian Portuguese and English were the first phrases said to the students, informing them to organize themselves in a circle in the middle of the cafeteria. In alignment with culturally responsive curricula that affirms the importance of content taught in the language of students (Brown, 2004; Phuntsog, 1999; Villegas & Lucas, 2002), I consistently offered commands in Brazilian Portuguese followed by English. The students were familiar with this practice and ran to the center of the cafeteria.

Once a circle formed, we stood together facing the United Capoeira Association banner, Brazilian and Pan-African flags. It was our custom to begin each session by recognizing the history of Capoeira in Brazil alongside the ancestral lineages of Africa. I reminded the students that we acknowledge the roots of Capoeira by a call and response that included me stating the word *Axé* that loosely translates to life, energy, and affirmation followed by a connecting element to the origin hypotheses. They were reminded to reply with Axé.

As we began our session on that Monday in November, I started the call and response with, "Axé Afrika!" The students responded, "Axé!" Then I said, "Axé Brasil." They replied, "Axé!" To conclude, I recognized slavery where Capoeira began to blossom with the phrase, "las senzalas do Brasil," which translates into English as, the slave quarters of Brazil. In unison, the students said, "Axé!" This practice of beginning class with honoring the historical components of Capoeira was borrowed from the partnership I formed with another local group while serving as the Marcus Chavez Elementary school's gym teacher.

My next words to the students were, "Vamos fazer trinta flexões; we are going to do thirty push-ups." Jermaine said, "What?" His response was in response to adding more push-ups, because I typically only assigned between ten and twenty push-ups. I was feeling generous on that day and decided to increase my normal request! After they performed fifteen, I told them to stop and sit down for a set of fifteen abdominal crunches. Following the push-ups and crunches, I instructed everyone to, "Sit criss-cross applesauce," which is a phrase often used among elementary school teachers to ask students to sit down on the floor with their legs crossed.

## Roda Real Talk Continues

After asking Michael and Wesley to refocus their energy in class, I asked the group about what they had to eat for lunch. Jeff was the first one among The Fellas to respond. He said, "I had chicken, fries, and a little bit of the green beans. They were nasty. I hate vegetables." I responded, "Ok the chicken is a good source of protein. Potatoes can be healthy when they aren't fried. They give your body iron. Although, you may not like to eat your vegetables, they are important in helping you grow strong. Eating healthy foods can help you do better in school and Capoeira." A few other students responded with the food they consumed for lunch, and I offered a similar response to Jeff.

Jermaine told me that he had the chicken with some ketchup for lunch. He threw away the milk, green beans, and the fries. "The green beans and fries were cold," he shared as his reason for deciding to throw them away. Similar to Jeff, I told him the chicken is an excellent source of protein critical for building strong muscle. I also told him about the importance of not wasting food. Other students commented about eating an orange for lunch. When I asked Jermaine about the orange offered to him, he said, "I don't like oranges."

Jermaine's comment about the oranges led me to a brief discussion about the limited access to stores with fresh fruits and vegetables in the underserved communities my students called home. These *food deserts*, neighborhoods without affordable healthy food options, are an increasing problem among environments where lower-income people of color live in the United States (Raja, Ma, & Yadav, 2008; Shannon, 2014; Walker, Keane, & Burke, 2010). I asked Jermaine if he ate oranges at home, and he said, "Sometimes, but we normally get food from the corner store and they don't sell oranges."

Without belaboring the point, I explained to Jermaine and the other students that it is important to eat fruit and vegetables when possible. I recognized their enjoyment of hot chips, candy, and other options available at local gas stations and corner stores, but I also encouraged them to look for healthier choices. The Marcus Chavez Elementary cafeteria staff served fruit or vegetables with every meal, but they could not force the students to eat it during lunch or other mealtimes. Through our conversations about nutrition and exercise, I asked students to take advantage of the healthier food options available at lunch and snack time.

Maintaining the circle formed for the roda, I shifted the focus of the class from talk to movement. "Let's do 15 more push-ups and crunches," I said. The students vocalized their lack of desire for more exercise with an exaggerated breath followed by, "Ugh," and then they complied. A few students demonstrated improper form and so I modeled the correct way to do a push-up and an abdominal crunch.

When everyone finished the exercises, I told them that being in shape consists of eating healthy foods and staying active. I continued by explaining how in our communities, many people are unable to, or don't have access to the resources needed to maintain a healthy body weight. While looking into their eyes, I said we can live full lives. I stressed how crucial it is to develop healthy bodies, to do our best in Capoeira, in school, and in our communities. With only thirty-five minutes remaining for class, I decided to end the discussion and get the students moving.

## Ginga

I began with Ginga, the physical movement that consists of stepping back and forth in a triangular motion while using your arms for protection. I reminded students that Ginga is the base movement for everything we do in Capoeira. Each class began with a review of Ginga as a warm-up exercise and to sharpen it as a foundational movement.

I pressed play on my iPod, and as soon as everyone could hear the Capoeira music coming from the portable speaker, I asked the students to follow my lead, "Put your right leg back with your right arm up to protect your face. Step to the line and switch. Put your left leg back and left arm up." In unison, the class began to sway to the rhythm of the music.

By November, we held multiple sessions of the after-school program, yet some students continued to struggle with the coordination required for the execution of Ginga. They demonstrated confusion about how and when to place their arm in front and when to step back with the corresponding leg. While I walked around the room to offer more individualized instruction, I asked Steve to lead the class.

With a smile on his face, Steve stepped into the leadership role of performing Ginga while the students followed his lead in four separate lines. I told the students, "We are not stopping until this track stops playing. It's about five minutes, and I know that you can make it!" As I corrected Jeff's form, he asked me "Why do we always begin with Ginga?" I asked Steve to stop.

Addressing the class, I said, "Jeff asked me about the purpose of Ginga and why we begin class with it." I asked the students, "Can anyone answer this question?" When no one responded, I said, "Ginga is how some argue that Queen Nzingha from Angola signed her name when writing the Portuguese (Taylor, 2012). She felt compelled to sign her name as Ginga because it sounded like a king's name. The Portuguese did not respect women leaders. We begin class with Ginga to honor her legacy, and because it is the base for all the moves, you will learn." I told Steve to resume and continue for another two minutes while I adjusted Jeff and the other students who struggled with Ginga.

For another fifteen minutes, we worked on Ginga variations, several primary kicks, and evasive techniques. Some of the exercises were performed in lines with me at the head of the class demonstrating the proper form. Others were taught by students to work together in partnerships and small groups. With ten minutes remaining for class, I asked students to return to the roda.

## Music and Play

I pulled out the instruments at the start of class, but I was unable to organize them before the students arrived. It took me five minutes to place the four instruments in position to provide instruction and to review a song. As indicated in the previous chapter's description, the central Capoeira instruments that lead the roda, include a berimbau, atabaque, ago-go, reco-reco, and a pandeiro. These instruments alongside the Capoeiristas who play them compose the *bateria*, or musical band responsible for the selection of songs and tempo that guide the movement of the two players inside and others who surround the circle, roda. On Monday, I decided to use the berimbau, atabaque, pandeiro, and reco-reco instruments for instruction.

By November, all the students were familiar with the instruments. I grabbed the berimbau and asked Michael, Wesley, and another student to join me in the folding chairs I placed at the top of the roda to play the other instruments. With the other students sitting in a circle, with their legs folded on the brown tile floor of the cafeteria, I asked the students to repeat after me, "Oi sim, sim, sim, oi não, não, não." The students repeated those Brazilian Portuguese words that translate to, "Oh yes, yes, yes, oh no, no, no."

After hearing the students follow my lead with the chorus of the song, I began to sing the remaining lyrics created by an unknown author and sung in every Capoeira school.

> Oi sim, sim, sim, oi não, não, não
> Oi sim, sim, sim, oi não, não, não
>
> Mas hoje tem amanhã não
> Mas hoje tem amanhã não
>
> Oi sim, sim, sim, oi não, não, não
> Oi sim, sim, sim, oi não, não, não
>
> Olha bizado de Lampião
> Olha bizado de Lampião
>
> Oi sim, sim, sim, oi não, não, não
> Oi sim, sim, sim, oi não, não, não

This song was one of the first songs I taught the students, and I wanted to see if they remembered its meaning. I asked the students, "Who remembers what this song means in English?" One student replied, and said "it means yes and no." By nodding my head, I confirmed the response and went further.

"It is a song that is about appreciating what you have today because tomorrow it could be gone. Hence the lyrics, Oi sim, sim, sim, oi não, não, não translates to oh yes, yes, yes, oh no, no, no. Mas hoje tem amanhã não, means, but today, there is no tomorrow." With three minutes remaining in class I said, "This song is important because it reminded the enslaved Africans who created Capoeira to appreciate their lives during a difficult time. It also references a legend, Lampião, who similar to Robin Hood stole from the rich to give to the poor."

Looking at the bateria, I instructed them to follow my lead and play the instruments while singing. As the person with the berimbau, I began to play first. Michael followed me with the pandeiro. Wesley soon after scraped the bamboo wood of the reco-reco, and another student joined in with the atabaque. In the call and response tradition of singing in the roda, I began to sing, "Oi sim, sim, sim, oi não, não, não." The students repeated my words in unison while clapping to the rhythm of the instruments. We didn't sound perfect, but I was happy with the progress made that day.

To conclude our class, I asked students to keep the circle and stand. As a ritual in alignment with the United Capoeira Association tradition, we ended with a song that roughly translates to English as, "Long live the senior teacher who taught me Capoeira and long live Capoeira." The song consists of a call and response with the teacher leading and the students following. It went like this,

Me: Iê viva meu Mestre
Students in Unison: Iê viva meu Mestre, camara
Me: Iê, que me ensinou
Students in Unison: Iê, que me ensinou, camara
Me: Iê a Capoeira
Students in Unison: Iê a Capoeira, camara.

As we finished this song acknowledging Capoeira and the senior teachers, other Marcus Chavez Elementary students began to walk into the cafeteria for their afternoon snack. I asked The Fellas, and several other students to help me return the tables to their position and place the instruments in the storage closet. The next day, I reminded Michael, Jermaine, Jeff, Wesley, and Steve is the day we are scheduled to conduct the focus group interview.

## Tuesday's Focus Group Interviews

The after-school program only took place on Mondays and Wednesdays of each week during the 2015–2016 academic year. On the other days of some weeks, I went to the school to conduct classroom observations or to complete scheduled interviews with administrators, students, and teachers. On a Tuesday following a Monday after school session, I held a focus group interview with Michael, Steve, Jeff, Wesley, and Jermaine.

With the intention to not disrupt learning in the classroom, I scheduled our focus group interview for after school. With the help of the administrative assistant, I reserved a vacant office space to ensure the privacy of our conversation. My goal was to get the students to talk openly about their experiences at Marcus Chavez Elementary. I wanted to learn more about how they connected with the curriculum taught in their classes and how they saw Capoeira impacting their experiences as a student and other life experiences as young Black males living in Chicago.

On the day of the interviews, I arrived at the school at 3:15 PM. Contrary to the previous day, the administrative assistant was sitting at her desk when I came and opened the door as soon as I pressed the doorbell. I walked into the school, and I could tell by the look on her face, that she was surprised to see me. The after-school program only took place on Monday and Wednesday afternoons. It was not often that she saw me on Tuesdays.

I explained to her that I was there to interview a couple of students. She smiled and said, "Ok, I thought for a second that I had my days mixed up!" I returned her smile and proceeded to the students' classrooms. Michael, Wesley, Jermaine, Steve, and Jeff were in their final periods of the day when I arrived. I needed to wait an additional ten minutes before I could take them from their classes for the interview.

With a copy of their class schedules, provided to me by an administrator, I knew where to find them on Tuesday afternoons. Michael, Wesley, Jermaine, Steve, and Jeff were in a class called *Politics 100*. It was one of the classes offered as part of Marcus Chavez Elementary school's culturally responsive curriculum, designed to increase social consciousness and to encourage students into pursuing social justice activism. The course began with the identification of a challenge in the students' communities and throughout each quarter, solutions were proposed, and steps were taken toward the implementation of remedies. From prior classroom observations, I was familiar with the course and the curriculum.

After giving the teachers a few moments to wrap up their lessons, I went around to pick up the students. When The Fellas saw me, they knew I was there for the interviews we prearranged and confirmed the day before. The teachers needed a reminder but released everyone without a problem. I walked the five students to a private office, closed the door, and began the interview.

We started with my preliminary statement about the importance of maintaining confidentiality. I read from the interview script, "Although we ask everyone in the group to respect everyone's privacy and confidentiality, and not to identify anyone in the group or repeat what is said during the group discussion, please remember that other participants in the group may accidentally disclose what is said." The students nodded at me in a gesture to say they understood and I proceeded with the opening statement for the interview after pressing record on my device.

I said, "I want you to talk about the problem that you talked about during your Politics 100 class," to initiate our conversation. Jeff, the oldest among the study's participants, responded first, "We chose teen pregnancy." I asked, "How did you choose teen pregnancy? Did the teacher provide a list or did the class choose it on their own?"

Jeff offered additional details about the process of how they decided to explore the challenge of teen pregnancies in his community. "What we did was, we thought about it as a group. We split up into groups, and we each came up with our own individual topic. We had to research it a little bit and present on how this topic mattered in our communities. Then we presented it to our class and the class voted on each topic. It was between HIV and child abuse. Then teen pregnancy sprouted from those two." Jeff's comments reveal how Politics 100 empowered the students to select a topic of focus. Among the students' groups, they identified HIV and child abuse as challenges impacting their communities, but from the discussion that stemmed from the voting results, they chose teen pregnancy.

To gain further insight into why the seventh grade decided to pursue teen pregnancy as a topic, I asked Jeff why he believed that teen pregnancy was an important topic. Jeff responded, "I think that it is worthy to discuss because sometimes many teens undergo a lot of pressure from either their peers or their parents. They may not be receiving a lot of attention. It's not always the parents' fault, even though most of the pressure is put on the teen themselves. It's like some teens just see it as a way to get to relax after a long time of stress and things. And sometimes, you don't feel as whole by yourself so you seek out a man and a baby." It's important to note from this quote that Jeff believes teenagers have sex, due to peer pressure and strained relationships with parents. In his comments, "You seek out a man and a baby," is an indication that he sees teen pregnancy as primarily a problem for young women. Either he didn't understand that males are also required to produce children, or he chose to ignore their role in the relationship.

Jeff was the first to speak among the group, and the only student among my participants in the seventh grade. While he shared about teen pregnancy, Steve, Michael, Wesley, and Jermaine listened with a sincere intensity. As the oldest among The Fellas, Jeff appeared to command an unspoken amount of respect. Each grade level took a version of the Politics 100 course, but it differed with regards to the classroom topic.

When I directly asked Wesley and Jermaine about their Politics 100 experiences, they replied with a cacophony of responses. Without any regards for what each other had to say, they blurted a list of topics, "Race, gender, kingdoms, right now we are talking about Africa, Mali, Ghana, desserts, cabanas, oceans, rivers, lakes, Nile rivers." From these responses, it was clear to me that they were listing topics discussed in their international studies course. I reiterated that I wanted to learn more about their Politics 100 experiences to which they said, "Oh bullying."

When I probed why Wesley and Jermaine's class believed bullying was an important issue in school, Jermaine was the first to respond. He said, "Some people don't get enough attention at home." Wesley replied, "There are some [bullies] that are jealous of them or they want to be like them." Jermaine and Wesley offered me explanations of why they thought some students decided to practice bullying behaviors. According to Jermaine, students choose to practice bullying behaviors due to a lack of attention received in their home environments. Wesley suggested that bullying was the result of jealousy.

Steve and Michael's Politics 100 class did not choose jealousy or teen pregnancy for their topics of interest, instead, they decided to discuss sexual violence. Michael's first words after admitting the sixth-grade selected sexual violence included, "I don't like that topic." I asked him, "Why not?" He replied, "I mean there are only a few of them, but like um … They are very inappropriate about that topic." I asked for clarity with a follow-up question, "What, they [other students] aren't mature enough to talk about that stuff?" Michael confirmed and said, "Yes, they just laugh."

As we continued, they talked about a group of sixth-grade boys unable to have a serious conversation about sexual violence. Steve said they laughed about the issue and dismissed it as a problem for girls. In Steve's words, "Some of the boys, they laugh. They say it's just about the girls. Like the campaign, they say most of it is just going to be about the girls." Steve expressed how some boys in his class undermined the impact of sexual violence on males and females.

To verify that I understood Michael and Steve's perspectives on sexual violence, I clarified with a question and statement. I said, "But you all know that's not the case. You understand that boys can be a victim of sexual violence like a girl can right?" In unison, they replied "Yes." Dominant narratives that support hierarchical privileges and gendered oppression may suggest that young men are less common targets of rape or other sexual offenses (Collins, 2000; Haskins & Singh, 2015). With this understanding of the dominant narratives and intersectionality, I felt compelled to verify with Michael and Steve that they understand the social construct of gender often influences slanted perceptions of sexual violence victims.

To understand the solutions proposed in Politics 100 to address the students' concerns of their community, I asked about the campaign component of the course. According to Jermaine, "1 out of 6 boys will be bullied by the age of 24. There are a lot of LGBT students getting bullied and there is also cyberbullying." Before I could respond, Wesley said, "What is LGBT?" Jermaine answered, "You know Lesbian, Bi-sexual, Gay, Transgender. Remember, we watched that *Law and Order* episode in a class where the boy was transgender, her, I mean she, was getting bullied and then pushed off the bridge ..." Jermaine continued to talk for five minutes about other video clips used in class to illustrate how bullying impacted people from a variety of sexual identities. Wesley said, "Awe ok I remember now," and as Jermaine finished his explanation, I took their attention back to my question.

I asked, "What are you doing within the school to impact bullying?" Jermaine replied, "We are doing peace circles." I asked, "What is a peace circle?" Wesley answered, "A peace circle is when all the classes gather around and talk about their feelings on a certain topic." To understand if the actions taken in school were also applied in their neighborhoods, I followed up and asked if they tried to use peace circles in their communities. Wesley said, "I want to [implement peace circles], but no. One time, I saw someone got shot right in front of my house. I was right there when I came home from my grandma house. There were two fire trucks, ten police cars and a lot of lights. We had to go through the backyard, just to get back to my house."

These comments by Wesley reveal that the use of peace circles is effective at school to address bullying, but remain difficult to implement in his neighborhood where violence continues to influence the quality of life.

When I redirected the question toward Steve about the sixth-grade class' campaign to influence sexual violence, he offered a response that reflected school and community initiatives. Steve said, "We talked about doing protests for sexual violence, fundraising or like organizing a talk with teachers or other organizations. We had like three organizations come in and talk to us about sexual violence and tell us about like who they work with." From Steve's words, it appears that his teacher created a relationship with community organizations that work to impact sexual violence. These organizations came to the school and presented their findings to Steve and his classmates. At the time of this interview, Steve's class planned to organize protests and public discussion to bring more awareness to sexual violence interventions.

With regards to teen pregnancy, I was curious about the seventh-grade class' approach to influence change. Jeff stated, "I know that in my father's side of the family, my grandmother had her first child at seventeen. It was like really hard for her because she had to provide for a child. This happened in another country." Before allowing him to continue, I asked, "Where did this happen?" He said, "The Bahamas and the man who she had a child with was a grown man. He was a very intimidating person, so she had to flee the country without the child." Jeff continued to speak about his family's experiences with teen pregnancies for three minutes. It was clear to me that a part of his class's actions included having conversations with family members about the impact of having children at a young age. Jeff's comments did not reveal what additional steps were proposed to influence behavioral changes.

Through my efforts to connect the after-school program to the Politics 100 course, I asked the students how they saw the practice of Capoeira aligning with the efforts to bring awareness and influence change. My specific question with regards to sexual violence was, "How do you think Capoeira could help to bring awareness to issues around sexual violence?" For clarity, I added, "If it can, I'm not sure that it can, and it's ok if you don't see Capoeira as playing a role. I just want to hear your thoughts on the use of Capoeira as part of your efforts to make an impact." As the students' Capoeira teacher, I attempted to eliminate as much bias as possible from the interview with my choice of language for the question and follow-up statement. Phrases such as, "It's ok if you don't see Capoeira," were used to help students feel unrestricted in how they could express themselves.

Michael was first to respond to the potential use of Capoeira in regards to the resources used to influence sexual violence. He said, "I think it [Capoeira] could. Well, I mean people could teach Capoeira throughout different places. And like throughout the Capoeira class like we do in the club, we could talk about different things we learned in school. We could talk about things like sexual violence in the community. We could bring awareness to them through Capoeira." Michael saw Capoeira as an activity that could bring people together and provide the opportunities for dialogue about sexual violence. It was clear to me that his response received influence by the model he participated in as part of the after-school program.

Steve's perspective was different from Michael, but it did reflect an essential component of Capoeira's potential taught in the gym class and now transferred to the after-school program. In Steve's voice, he added, "I think Capoeira could help by self-defense because usually someone that becomes a victim of sexual assault is kidnapped or taken somewhere where they are not supposed to go. So, if someone tries to kidnap them, they could use something that will help them get a chance to run." Although Steve was unable to acknowledge how often sexual violence occurs in a familiar environment of the victim by a family member or friend, it is interesting to note the difference in his perspective from Michael. He saw Capoeira as a preventative tool potential victims could use to defend themselves; whereas Michael viewed it as a resource to influence sexual violence awareness.

With regards to Capoeira and teen pregnancy, I asked Jeff a similar question to Michael and Steve. My question had two parts, "What impact has Capoeira made on your experiences in school? What role do you see Capoeira playing in the solutions to influence teen pregnancies?" With this two-fold question, I hoped to gain insight into how Capoeira influenced Jeff's experiences and if whether he saw it as a resource similar to Steve and Michael.

Jeff's attendance in the after-school program was not consistent throughout the 2015–2016 academic year. He would often use after school to receive tutoring on his homework or to attend other clubs. More than others, I was curious about his response due to how I perceived a lack of enthusiasm from him about Capoeira.

To my question about the impact of Capoeira on his student experiences and its role in influencing teen pregnancy, Jeff offered a surprising response, "I think that Capoeira is a positive thing, because of the fact that it introduces the achievement of other cultures from around the world. The fact that it can be brought to you and you can learn it from other people who have um, learned it well. You can feel more energized by practicing with another person who is performing Capoeira with you. The fact that it gives you something to do. I think that people need something to do, so they don't start doing things that their morals don't consider good or bad. I feel that it is a positive thing for me." I was impressed by the maturity of Jeff's comments and how he identified Capoeira as a positive activity with the potential to help young people from "Doing things that their morals don't consider good." Jeff appreciated Capoeira because it offered him a healthy physical outlet. In his words, it helped occupy idle time that students might use otherwise to engage in sexual behaviors leading to teen pregnancies.

After Michael, Steve, and Jeff responded to my question about the influence of Capoeira, I looked at Jermaine and Wesley. They returned the smile I gave them with a look of concern. I could tell that they were growing restless and I needed to quickly ask them my last question, before allowing the group to leave. Our focus group interview began at 3:35 PM, and it was now 4:15 PM. After a full day at school, The Fellas appeared tired.

My question for Jermaine and Wesley resembled what I asked Michael, Steve, and Jeff. "Do you believe that Capoeira can play any role in impacting bullying?" Unlike Jeff, Jermaine and Wesley were active in the after-school program. They participated in the, "roda real talks," and appeared to enjoy the physical and musical components of Capoeira class.

Jermaine was the first to speak followed by Wesley about how they viewed Capoeira in their class's campaign against bullying, "No, well maybe Capoeira can make the bully stronger," said Jermaine. Wesley responded, "No it can make the person who is getting bullied fight back." Jermaine, replied, "Capoeira helps me beat up people!" The group laughed, and Michael said, "You don't beat up people." From Jermaine and Wesley's perspective, they saw Capoeira in terms of its ability to provide self-defense techniques. They did not see it as a resource for awareness about bullying. It was a martial art to them that could either give the bully or the victim enhanced skills to fight.

Before I let the group leave to the cafeteria for the afternoon snack, I asked one additional question. My goal was to hear their perspectives on how Capoeira influenced positive self-awareness. The question began with, "Ok we all know that Capoeira began among enslaved Africans, right?"; the group's responses included, "Yes" and "yea." I continued with, "Well how does practicing it make you feel about yourself, given that it began in slavery among Black people who were similar to your ancestors? Does it make you feel like you can do anything given the history?" Multiple responses came my way as I finished this statement and question.

The Fellas replied to me with a series of: "Yes"; "I feel strong"; "it makes me feel strong"; "I have pride." Due to the importance of the question, I prompted the group to speak more about their experiences and feelings about Capoeira. With the intention to minimize bias in their responses I said, "Well tell me more about you feel, and I want you to be honest. Do you enjoy it? No matter how you feel about Capoeira, just open-up to me and let me know your thoughts. Whether you love it or hate it, let's talk for a few minutes about Capoeira." These additional comments soliciting more input appeared to resonate with The Fellas.

Steve was the first one to offer a formal response, "It's something that I enjoy. I like the elements of the music, culture, and the martial art. The history of Capoeira of how it began as a dance to fight others. So yes, how it gets passed on from generation to generation is inspiring." Language such as "inspiring," found in Steve's response is an indicator that he appreciated Capoeira, and the after-school program provided him with a valuable resource. When I asked Jermaine, who sat next to Steve what he thought about Capoeira, he simply replied, "The same thing."

To extract more of Jermaine's thoughts, I asked him to give me more details about how he connected with Capoeira, "Yea, because in Capoeira the history behind how it came. You know how they thought it was just a dance and how they [enslaved Africans] used Capoeira to fight against them [Portuguese]. How they used it to get freedom and now it gets passed on from generation to today." In Jermaine's words, it is feasible to observe that he connected with Capoeira through the history of its development in Brazil. His references to how the enslaved Africans camouflaged it as a dance, but used it in the fight for freedom.

From the other group member's brief responses, I understood they enjoyed Capoeira and it influenced how they perceived their physical abilities. Comments such as, "I feel strong," and "It makes me strong," came from the mouths of Michael, Wesley, and Jeff when I pleaded with them to offer some additional input. Michael expanded and said, "Well I don't know. Oh, it did help me meet new people, and I learned how to move faster." It was apparent that The Fellas had reached their breaking point with regards to the interview, so I did not probe further on that day.

From the interviews, I learned that the boys enjoyed Capoeira and viewed it as a resource to assist the efforts outlined in their Politics 100 course. It was difficult to assess whether they internalized the history of Capoeira's role as a tool of resistance to influence how they viewed their potential as young people racialized as Black in America. With this understanding, I returned on subsequent days for the after-school program determined to create more meaningful relationships with The Fellas by offering critical dialogues and instruction of Capoeira's philosophies, physical movements, music, and rituals. I was also curious about the proposed community work established in Politics 100.

## Wednesday Capoeira Classes

On Wednesday, I arrived for the after-school program with an intention to motivate the students and to encourage critical thinking about their identities.

To avoid any delays in getting started, I organized the tables in the cafeteria and the instruments for class before the students arrived. Of the twenty-one enrolled in Capoeira, only nine showed up on Wednesday. Jeff wasn't feeling well and sat on the floor for the entire session.

On that day, the nine students attended appeared to be in a unique mood. They came into the cafeteria, and instead of waiting for class to begin, they chased each other playing tag. It wasn't until I reminded them of the fifty push-ups each consequence, that they decided to relax and follow protocol. Once they were calm, a teacher came into the cafeteria and asked about visiting me at the university to observe one of my classes. We talked for a few minutes, and in that time the students went back to playing tag.

"Ok let's do fifty push-ups," is how our class finally started. None of the students could complete fifty push-ups without taking multiple breaks. At 4:20 pm, we started our discussion in the roda. With the Thanksgiving holiday in a few weeks, I asked the students about their plans for the break and why they believed we needed a day called Thanksgiving. Michael said, "the day is about giving thanks." Steve said, "Not really," and Wesley recited a poem from a class that complicated Michael's interpretation of the holiday.

Jermaine replied to my question about the significance of Thanksgiving with, "It's about murder and the settlers." Although I was familiar with the perspective of European Pilgrims sitting peacefully together with First Nation people to share a meal, I was aware of the counter-narrative that Jermaine shared with the group. He spoke to the understanding that Europeans arrived on the shores of, "The New World" with guns, gold, and the intention to colonize. I was confident that Jermaine, Michael, and Wesley's responses were reflective of the culturally responsive curriculum at Marcus Chavez Elementary designed to encourage critical thinking.

After our brief discussion, I decided to revisit two self-defense movements in the remaining time allocated for class. The first was a kick called *mei-lua de frente* which is a crescent kick that translates in English to half-moon from the front. *Cocorinha* which is a defense response involving squatting low to the ground, while keeping one hand in position to protect the head, was the second movement I demonstrated and refined with the students. As partners and in a line formation we drilled these simple self-defense tactics.

At the end of the class, I asked everyone to make a roda. We did not have time to play instruments or sing a song, but I wanted to address the behavioral problems that prevented the timely start of class. I talked about the importance of behaving with maturity and internalizing discipline to do the right thing even when it is difficult. While looking in the eyes of the young people, I told each of them to come to the next session prepared with a focused mind and body.

We ended our time together with the closing call and response that the United Capoeira Association uses to recognize senior teachers, Capoeira, and community. I did not have a chance to explore identity as originally planned.

## Thursday's Academic and Social Observations

I came to Marcus Chavez Elementary early on Thursday to collect observations of the students. I intended to attend the students' Politics 100, math, and lunch periods. I hoped to see the culturally responsive curriculum in practice and observe the students in a social environment. The interviews peaked my interest to visit the students' classes, examine pedagogy, and identify any differences to how they behaved with me in Capoeira.

Ms. Osuna's Politics 100 course, where Steve and Michael were students, was the first class I decided to observe. Through my conversations with Ms. Osuna, I learned she was passionate about education and the preparation of students to impact social justice causes. Although she was not born in Mexico, it was clear to me Ms. Osuna carried great affection for her family abroad and community in Chicago. When I arrived to observe her class, she greeted me with a smile and told me to take any available seat. I chose to sit at a small green circular table located near a wooden bookcase in the east corner of the classroom.

While she gathered her supplies and began to write on the whiteboard in front of the class, I took note of the classroom's setting. The floor of the classroom had blue carpet and along the wall were posters from different marches organized by students, teachers, and administrators at the school. Desks were arranged in three columns facing toward the white dry erase board attached to a green wall and adjacent to a large map of Africa. Ms. Osuna's desk was positioned in the rear of the classroom.

In addition to the posters hung from the wall, the classroom was decorated with images reflective of the students' cultural backgrounds. There were pictures of famous Black and Latinx civil rights' activists on each of the four walls. On the opposite wall to the whiteboard, was a tact piece of African fabric. Next, to Ms. Osuna's desk, there was an 11 × 14 inch map of Chicago that highlighted the racial demographics of each community.

In addition to the culturally responsive décor, Ms. Osuna decorated the room with general academic items. On one of the walls was a sign titled, "The Writing Process," that explained the drafting, revising, and editing phases of completing an assignment. Displayed on the north wall with three large rectangular windows was a multiplication time table chart. Next to the chart was a vibrant 8.5 × 14.0-inch size school calendar. Ms. Osuna's classroom reflected her vision for the classroom which I interpreted as the preparation of students for academic success and equipping them with the knowledge of themselves in the world.

I choose the seat where I could observe Michael and Steve while also keeping an eye on the board where Ms. Osuna stood in authority. A guest presenter from a local community organization was in attendance on this Thursday I observed the class. Ms. Osuna began the subject with an introduction of the speaker and reminded the students, she expected them to display their best behavior.

The presenter began by explaining her organization's services to provide resources for people impacted by sexual violence. She talked about the importance of finding an adult who is deserving their trust. Statistics were offered to discuss the relevance of sexual abuse. Many of the students, including Michael, listened to hear every word that came from the speaker's mouth. Steve appeared disinterested and attempted to have side conversations with the student sitting next to him. I caught his eye a few times and mouthed the words, "Get it together." He stopped talking for a few moments and then resumed where he left off.

Ms. Osuna went to Steve and gently nudged him to show more respect for the guest speaker. His response to Ms. Osuna was similar to the one he gave me. He stopped for a minute and then resumed talking as if Ms. Osuna or I had said nothing at all. I took a note to speak with him after class. As the presenter wrapped up her brief presentation, she said, "Ok let's open up for some questions. I would like to hear one ridiculous question and one serious question."

Steve was the first to respond to the request for participation. His question was, "Have you ever been sexually assaulted?" The presenter did not appear disturbed by the directness of Steve's question. She responded, "Yes and that's why I do this work." Steve shook his head as an indicator that he understood, and appeared to listen more for the remainder of the class. Unlike Steve's displays of disrespect that included talking during the presentation, Michael sat in silence. Michael appeared engaged but did not make any statements or ask any questions.

Before leaving to observe Jermaine and Wesley in Math, I asked Ms. Osuna if it would be okay for me to speak with Steve in the hallway. She said yes, and Steve followed me out the classroom's gray set of double doors. I told Steve that I was disappointed in his behavior and that I expected more from him in class. He replied with an excuse claiming that it was the students sittting next to him. I reminded Steve that I was in class and witnessed the disrespect he showed the guest speaker.

Steve put his head down, and it was evident that he felt shame. I told him that my expectations for him to stay focused in Capoeira class should also apply to his performance in academic subjects. While maintaining direct eye contact, I said, "You are a leader who has the intelligence, ability, and discipline to do well in school." Steve nodded his head, and we continued to talk for another five minutes about expectations for his behavior moving forward. I opened the doors to Ms. Osuna's classroom, gave him a firm hand-shake, and told him that I would check on him occasionally to ensure he stayed on track in class.

Jermaine and Wesley's math class was right next door to Ms. Osuna's classroom. Mrs. Smith was the math teacher and I didn't have as much of a relationship with her as I shared with Ms. Osuna. She was a new teacher and carried a reputation for being one of the more strict teachers on staff. Before entering her classroom, I knocked on the wooden door with twelve glass panels and waited for permission to enter.

Mrs. Smith opened the door with a smile and welcomed me inside. I told her that I was there to record observations for the research project and she said, "Ok that's fine." Similar to Ms. Osuna, she instructed me to take any available seat. I decided to sit near her desk where I could see the entire class. In many ways, Mrs. Smith's classroom resembled Ms. Osuna's decorations with regards to prominent figures in the history of Black and Latinx communities.

From the amount of student artwork, posters, signs, and other decorative objects it was evident that Mrs. Smith put a lot of time and energy into orga-nizing her classroom. It was a larger classroom than Ms. Osuna's room. The class schedule, rules, and a whiteboard where Mrs. Smith taught math were displayed on a bright yellow wall. In every corner of the room, there appeared samples of the students' work, colorful shapes labeled as triangles, squares, circles, octagons, and others.

Of the many signs found on the walls several stood out among the rest. There was a large display of Marcus Chavez Elementary school's "Pillars of

Justice." The pillars included language such as "Speaking up, Positive action, Curiosity, and Respect." Another memorable poster displayed "Problem-solving Checklist." Among the items on the checklist, included directions such as "Write the problem, read the problem twice, think of a strategy to use." A sign that read "Rockin Behavior," in the shape of a guitar, served as the classroom behavior chart. It was on the front wall of the classroom as a reminder of the students' conduct status.

On the green wall behind Mrs. Smith's desk were the words, "Classroom Helpers." The available positions included: class monitor, homework monitor, attendance monitor, maintenance crew, and personal assistant. Jermaine and Wesley's names did not appear next to any of the classroom helpers. Near Mrs. Smith's desk there was also a wooden bookcase with blue milk crates filled with the students' binders. Just to the left of the green wall and Mrs. Smith's desk were four large rectangular windows. The light that came in from the outside illuminated the blue carpet on the floor and gave the room a warm feeling that seemed conducive to learning.

There were a couple of indicators that supported the idea that Mrs. Smith was one of the more strict teachers at Marcus Chavez Elementary. On the outside of her desk, were the words "Class Rules." The rules included, "Do your best work at all times, respect your surroundings, respect others' thoughts, opinions, and questions." As indicated the second set of rules were displayed on the main wall with the whiteboard; they included, "Be mindful of those around you, work together, complete each task, stay focused." The reiteration of the rules in multiple places throughout the classroom affirmed Mrs. Smith's high expectations for the students' performances. She was tough, but not unreasonable.

Jermaine and Wesley sat on opposite sides of the classroom. Mrs. Smith told the students, "We are beginning with a two-minute drill competition to complete this worksheet. Your grade is based on the number of problems you answer correctly in this two-minute period." Jermaine and Wesley sat quietly in their seats. Mrs. Smith assigned one of the girl students who sat near the front of the class to hand out the worksheets.

As the students received the assignment, Mrs. Smith said, "Do not turn it over and begin until I tell you to start." Jermaine and Wesley played with their pencils in anticipation. Similar to the other students, they did not talk. When the last student received the worksheet, Mrs. Smith said, "I'm starting the timer, and you may begin now!"

When the two-minute timer went off, students were told to exchange papers and to grade each other's responses. Everyone participated in the assignment because for them it was a game. Through this brief competition, Mrs. Smith made math fun. I looked at the questions on the worksheet, and they included simple addition, subtraction, some simple multiplication, and a few division problems. Mrs. Smith used this interactive tool as a warm-up activity before beginning the lesson for that class.

The class worked on the order of operations for the remaining forty minutes. Jermaine did not say a word throughout Mrs. Smith's instruction. Wesley talked near the end of the class when he asked for clarity on the homework assignment. Other students spoke and interrupted the lesson. Mrs. Smith responded to these infractions without warning or a discussion and reduced their behavior points. At the end of Mrs. Smith's class, I decided to visit the lunchroom where Jeff's schedule indicated lunch.

Buzzing with the sound of children talking and playing, I could hear the seventh-grade class from the hallway outside Mrs. Smith's classroom. En route to the lunchroom were pictures of the children on the wall who the school honored for awards such as student of the month, perfect attendance, and honor roll. I walked to the lunchroom where I held Capoeira class and saw Jeff sitting at a table with his peers. He didn't appear to see me walk into the lunchroom and continued to smile and talk while he ate the school meal served for Thursday.

One of the boys at Jeff's table played with an iPad. As soon as Ms. Howard, the cafeteria worker, and lunch supervisor, saw the iPad, she asked the boy to put it away. He did, but only after he claimed he didn't know they couldn't have it during lunch, followed by whispering something else that I couldn't hear. Jeff didn't seem to appear phased by the incident with the iPad. He continued his conversation as if such infractions were commonplace during lunch.

On the menu for Thursday's lunch were apples, green beans, chicken sandwiches, and French fries. In the after-school program, I learned that Jeff was a vegetarian. His plate had the apple, green beans, and French fries. With the intention to not interfere with his normal interactions with his friends, I did not sit at his table. I sat at one of the tables near the windows and watched while he talked with his friends who appeared similar in temperament and confidence. As I wrapped up my field notes for Thursday, I began to think about the pending protest and how my work with Capoeira could lend support.

# References

Abc7 Chicago. (2018, July 12). *Chicago weather: Record breaking warmth possible this week.* Retrieved from http://abc7chicago.com/weather/chicago-weather-record-breaking-warmth-possible-thisweek/1064515/

Bell, D. (1987). *And we are not saved: The elusive quest for racial justice.* New York, NY: Basic Books.

Bell, D. (1992). *Faces at the bottom of the well: The permanence of racism.* New York, NY: Basic Books.

Brown, D. F. (2004). Urban teachers' professed classroom management strategies: Reflections of culturally responsive teaching. *Urban Education, 39*(3), 266–289.

Collins, P. (2000). *Black feminist thought: Knowledge, consciousness, and the politics of empowerment.* New York, NY: Routledge.

Dixson, A. D. (2006). The fire this time: Jazz, research and critical race theory. In A. D. Dixson, C. K. Rousseau, & J. K. Donnor (Eds.), *Critical race theory in education: All God's children got a song* (pp. 213–232). New York, NY: Routledge.

Haskins, H. N., & Singh, A. (2015). Critical race theory and counselor education pedagogy: Critical equitable training. *Counselor Education and Supervision, 54*(4), 288–302.

Parker, L., & Lynn, M. (2016). What's race got to do with it? Critical race theory's conflicts with and connections to qualitative research methodology and epistemology. In E. Taylor, D. Gillborn, G. Ladson-Billings (Eds.), *Foundations in critical race theory in education* (pp. 143–153). New York, NY: Routledge Taylor and Francis.

Phuntsog, N. (1999). The magic of culturally responsive pedagogy: In search of the genie's lamp in multicultural education. *Teacher Education Quarterly, 26*(3), 97–111.

Raja, S., Ma, C., & Yadav, P. (2008). Beyond food deserts: Measuring and mapping racial disparities in neighborhood food environments. *Journal of Planning Education and Research, 27*(4), 469–482.

Shannon, J. (2014). Food deserts: Governing obesity in the neoliberal city. *Progress in Human Geography, 38*(2), 248–266.

Solórzano, G. D., & Yosso, J. T. (2016). Critical race methodology: Counter-storytelling as an analytical framework for educational research. In E. Taylor, D. Gillborn, & G. Ladson-Billings (Eds.), *Foundations in critical race theory in education* (pp. 127–142). New York, NY: Routledge.

Villegas, A. M., & Lucas, T. (2002). Preparing culturally responsive teachers: Rethinking the curriculum. *Journal of teacher education, 53*(1), 20–32.

Walker, R. E., Keane, C. R., & Burke, J. G. (2010). Disparities and access to healthy food in the United States: A review of food deserts literature. *Health & place, 16*(5), 876–884.

Yosso, J. T. (2006). *Critical race counterstories along the Chicana/Chicano educational pipeline.* New York, NY: Routledge.

# · 5 ·

# RESISTANCE, SCHOOL
# CULTURE, AND CAPOEIRA

Mama mama can't you see?

What the police has done to me

They lock us up, they shoot us down
Patrol our hoods and bring us down

But ain't' no justice for Mike Brown
To be found on the ground
Afraid that I am Homan Square bound
And make the prisons Black and Brown
—Marcus Chavez Elementary teachers and students

## Introduction

On a January evening in 2016, we walked from Marcus Chavez Elementary
to the city's juvenile detention center. We chanted, sang songs of liberation,
and played Capoeira in protest to the police homicides of Michael Brown,
Rekia Boyd, Ronald "Ronnieman" Johnson, Laquan McDonald, and others.
It was a collective effort involving administrators, teachers, parents, and support staff to prepare the youth for this action. The local news, onlookers, and

others recorded the march. A social justice focused curriculum, weekly assemblies, an international studies program, after-school initiatives that included Capoeira, and other components of the school culture were responsible for that incredible moment. I followed the Marcus Chavez Elementary school students as we played our roles in the struggle to influence justice in Chicago and throughout the nation.

The unjustified killings of young people by the police began to receive increased attention in 2014. In Ferguson, Missouri there was Michael Brown, Baltimore's Freddie Gray, Chicago's Rekia Boyd, Cleveland's Tamir Rice, and other cases where police issued a vigilante form of justice in the streets (Bradley, Pulphus, & Jones, 2015; Lowery, 2016). Despite video and other evidence that the officers in these cases committed homicides, they were not found guilty of murder. Through these injustices, the criminal justice system affirmed that killing, rather than arresting, was an appropriate response when interacting with young people of color, more specifically, Black citizens of the United States. Similar to others, the students at Marcus Chavez Elementary did not accept the courts' rulings and instead decided they could do something to influence change.

In this chapter, I make use of staff interviews conducted during the school day and observation data collected from an evening march. With an intentional focus on the culturally responsive curriculum, it illuminates how the after-school program served as an extension of the lessons taught in the core academic subjects. I share how the school culture shaped administrative supervision, teacher preparation, and pedagogical methods. I begin with the march led by the children in their efforts to affect change and end with an analysis of how the school culture and curriculum influenced Capoeira class.

## Marching for Justice

Walking into the rear parking lot to enter the main campus doors of Marcus Chavez Elementary, it was possible to feel the energy of the students. Although it was January and cold outside, I was warm with anticipation for the march scheduled to begin at 4:30 PM. Instead of finding the students inside the school preparing for the protest, I was told by the executive administrative assistant that everyone was in front of the building for a pre-rally. The objectives of the demonstration included walking from the school to the city's juvenile detention center and bringing more awareness to police brutality.

I turned around and began to walk out the doors I entered. Then, I remembered that I wanted to bring a berimbau. My Capoeira instruments were stored in the closet of the cafeteria. Without a plan to organize a roda, where students could safely play Capoeira in the streets as part of the demonstration, I took the berimbau with me just in case there was an opportunity.

The night before the rally, I told my adult Capoeira students that we would not hold class. Instead of class, we agreed to support the school's efforts to engage in a direct action to influence police brutality. The culture that was a staple of my youth classes was also part of the evening and weekend training opportunities held for adults. Any person who trained under my leadership was made aware of Capoeira's history and presented with opportunities to discuss the contemporary consequences of individual and systemic racism. When I walked outside to the front of the school, several of my adult students were waiting for me and standing with the staff, teachers, and students.

Together we used our voices in a collective shout aimed toward justice for Rekia Boyd, Michael Brown, Eric Garner, and other unarmed victims of vigilante police justice. Michael, Jermaine, Wesley, Steve, Jeff, and about 75 other students from Marcus Chavez Elementary attended the pre-rally. Many of the students' parents were there to lend their voices, volunteer their time, and to increase efforts to keep the youth safe. The school's teachers and several administrators were present including, Mr. Steinsberg and Ms. Osuna who participated in interviews for this research. Local non-profit organizations, some notable Chicago activists, university students, and members of the community were also standing in front of the school and listening to the young leaders speak about their concerns.

A Black male student from the Gap Year program at Marcus Chavez Elementary began the rally with an explanation of the protest's purpose. He talked about police brutality, inequitable educational resources, and a racist criminal justice system. Another Black female student offered additional insight into the reasons for the protest while also relaying the importance of maintaining peace throughout the march, and thanking everyone for their support. These two students were among the oldest enrolled in the school and participated in Capoeira with me when it was offered as a gym class.

It was an honor for me to witness young people who started Capoeira, as part of the culturally responsive physical education program as third graders, now serve as social justice leaders ten years later. Their ability to articulate the necessity to protest reflected the strength of the curriculum at Marcus Chavez Elementary and the many adults who poured resources into them over the years. I was impressed with their maturity and confidence to discuss the importance of direct actions against injustices.

The rally lasted about twenty minutes before we began to march down the street and repeat chants. Students carried signs they made in class, with quotes that read, "No Justice, No Peace." One young person began a call and response with, "Turn up, don't turn down! There's a Rekia Boyd in every town." In unison, we repeated their words and continued to walk in the direction of the juvenile center.

Despite declaring that we were marching in part to the over-policing in communities of color, there were officers in place throughout the route blocking off intersections and creating boundaries that helped our group stay together. As we made our way through each neighborhood along the path to our destination we shouted, "No Justice! No Peace! No Racist Police!" It was irony to see the police presence patrolling the march. We continued with other provoking chants such as, "Back up, back up. We want freedom, freedom. All these dirty racist cops, we don't need 'em, need 'em." The youth exemplified courage through their repeating of anger provoking chants.

The coordinators of the protest, students, teachers, administrators, and local activists, planned a route with predetermined points where protestors could form a large circle in the middle of intersections to block all angles of traffic. At these locations, students danced, I played the berimbau while others added drums and tambourines. We had a jam session of resistance while looking in the eyes of state representatives, the police, of an unjust criminal justice system.

When we made it to one intersection, I decided it was a suitable location to play Capoeira with the students. I reminded myself that Capoeira was born in resistance and the desire for freedom kept it alive among oppressed people. With the berimbau in the hand of a trusted adult student, I instructed him to play and tapped the shoulder of another student to kneel and begin the game. We exchanged kicks and escapes as the students surrounded us in a vast roda shouting, "Whose streets? Our streets." It was a surreal moment to include the students and Capoeira as part of a protest designed to influence social justice.

We continued to walk the approximate three miles to the juvenile detention center. Throughout the march, I looked around me and saw the excitement on the children's faces despite the cold weather and a full day at school. When we arrived at the detention center, the two students who began the pre-rally started to speak again.

These two incredible young leaders initiated their comments with a song. "I can hear my brother crying, 'I can't breathe' Now I'm in the struggle, and I can't leave. Calling out the violence of the racist police. We ain't' gonna stop, til our people are free. No, we ain't' gonna stop til our people are free." The song was a salute to the life of Eric Garner who was killed by New York Police for allegedly loitering and selling loose cigarettes.

Before the students provided comments about their experiences in the march, they led one last chant. A Black male said "Ancestors watching, I know they watching. Ancestors watching, I know, I know." As I listened to these words I thought to myself, I hope the ancestors are watching and hearing our efforts to impact changes in the criminal justice system. Marcus Chavez Elementary and the Capoeira after-school program were not perfect entities, but we were trying to do our best to create measurable community change.

## Administrative Perspectives and School Culture

Mr. Steinsberg was a thirty-one year-old White male with eight years of experiences at the school.[1] He was one of the few male administrators at Marcus Chavez Elementary who also had experience as a classroom teacher. He began teaching first grade and over the years decided that joining the administrative wing of the school, was where he believed he could make a more significant contribution. As one of few male teachers employed at the school and a dynamic classroom leader, the principal prolonged his transition to Dean of Students. Mr. Steinsberg persisted with his plea over the course of his fifth year in the classroom, and eventually the school complied with reluctance to his promotion request.

Steinsberg was a champion of the school's mission, a strong supporter of the culturally responsive curriculum, and an active organizer of the march to the juvenile detention center. During our interview, I asked him about how he defines culturally responsive curriculum, a smile on his face appeared, and he replied,

> From my understanding, a lot of our faculty who are people of color, Black, in particular, know what a great curriculum looks like, however they have witnessed poor implementation. MCE'S approach to a culturally relevant curriculum is not just about perpetuating the status quo, a European centered curriculum where you only learn about four dead White presidents. The only time you talk about Black people is when they are mentioned as slaves. We focus on making our curriculum a closer more comprehensive reflection of the whole world. We pay special attention to honoring

who are students are, their race, their background and having it reflected in the literature they read. It's also about teaching them skills that can be applied.

From Steinsberg's lengthy response, it is evident that he shared an excep-
tional level of commitment to Marcus Chavez Elementary. With enthusiasm,
he discussed how the school's curriculum existed to interrupt "the status quo."
According to Steinsberg, a culturally responsive curriculum is the ability to
incorporate literature relevant to the historical and racial backgrounds of students, while fostering opportunities for application. Steinsberg's definition
of culturally responsive curriculum reflects how scholars interpret best practices to include cultural artifacts, common languages, and the tools to bridge
schools with home life (Gay, 2000; Irvine-Jordan, 1991; Sampson & Garrison-
Wade, 2011).

When I asked about the Politics 100 course in the interview with Steinsberg, I began by indicating how I had an opportunity to observe a class earlier in the school year. I continued with the question, "how is the culturally
responsive curriculum implemented in multiple subjects?" He said, yes, "I
believe that class is great because it builds the students' background knowledge. Things just don't exist right now in isolation. There are things in history that led up to the way things are now. If you don't look at that, then you
might oversimplify certain people and conditions in our community. We need
a social justice education to build that muscle, so our students are understanding power structures and institutional racism." Steinsberg believes the
strength of the school's curriculum is its ability to weave the past into the
contemporary challenges of students' communities. In alignment with critical
race theory, the curriculum acknowledges systemic racism and empowers students to raise their social consciousness.

To gain clarity on whether a culturally responsive approach impacted all
academic subjects, I asked a follow-up question. I said, "the tool of culturally
relevant curriculum, is that something used in every class. For example, let's
say the Spanish class is looking at something everyone decides is important
for that group of students. Is it carried over into science, math, English? Is it
interweaved that way?" Mr. Steinsberg paused and replied, "honestly, I believe
that's the vision. However, the reality is only as robust as the teacher's understanding of the subject and passion. So, you get a great teacher, and he or she
understands history and if they are really into this, race holds constant. It
really depends on the teacher's funds of knowledge and passion and are they
able to infuse that in." From Steinsberg's perspective, the use of culturally

responsive curriculum is encouraged in every subject, but its implementation is dependent on the ability of the teacher. He also acknowledges the importance of identity and critical dialogue by stating, "race holds constant," in subjects taught by teachers who understand history.

With the intention to fulfill the Marcus Chavez Elementary school's vision of culturally responsive curricula in every classroom, professional development focused on pedagogy and strategy. In Steinsberg's words, "We have some really great teachers who are still developing that consciousness on their own. In every science class, are you going to see it? I don't know. In every math class are you going to see this culturally relevant? I don't know. I would argue no, you are not going to see it in every class, but that's the goal, and with our professional development we are trying to show teachers. It's not, well this is Politics 100, that's when you tell students about who they are, and math is just for numbers. Our goal is to teach good instructional practices." Positive youth development theory encourages helping adolescents form healthy identities to support academic achievement (Byrd & Chavous, 2009; Murry, Berkel, Gaylord-Harden, Copeland-Linder, & Nation, 2011; Smith, Atkins, & Connell, 2003; Smith, Witherspoon, & Osgood, 2017; Youngblade et al., 2007). As an administrator, Steinsberg spoke to the culture at Marcus Chavez Elementary and highlighted the efforts to provide teachers with the skill set to offer quality academic instruction while also helping students form positive identities.

Steinsberg further discussed how different teachers bring their passions into the classroom and with more awareness can transform it into lessons more reflective of the students' backgrounds. He shared,

> I think all our teachers are capable and we just have to say here is the connection. Let's look for some statistics impacting their community and bring that into the classroom. In Spanish class, if you have a teacher who has a passion for the language component, then that will be the emphasis. Whereas if you have someone who understands the language and looks for social justice, then you will have a classroom with those types of conversations. I think this is the muscle that teachers really need to develop so they can do things at the same time.

Administrators encouraged teachers to use statistics or other forms of data reflective of the students' communities to establish connections with the academic subjects. In Steinsberg's perspective, the goal was to serve the learning objectives and the potential for application, "at the same time."

The ability to use a culturally responsive curriculum depends on the teacher's preparation. To provide teachers with the tools necessary to implement lesson plans aligned with the school's vision for the classroom, administrators encouraged staff to look for connections between their academic subjects and current events impacting the students' communities. Mr. Steinsberg witnessed how teachers made connections in his observation of science classes. He commented, "I've watched many lessons where they are honoring students' experiences and creating airspace to talk about it as part of the lesson. It's just not the science. They are talking about the Flint crisis and environmental racism. So, they are bringing in those kinds of concepts." Steinsberg is suggesting that teachers who can use their academic concentrations to make the curriculum relevant to students' lives can enhance academic performance. In this example, he discussed how science class was used as a resource to examine environmental racism while also providing a space to hear the students' voices.

To provide more evidence of how teachers implemented a culturally responsive curriculum, Steinsberg offered a specific example from another observation.

> Last year, I witnessed Ms. Taylor encourage students to do social justice science fair projects. They were kind of like sociology experiments. A student posed, do kids who possess memories of a racist event do better or worse on standardized tests? So, you start to get students who are trying to apply some of their skills to some of their interests.

Steinsberg highlights the culture at Marcus Chavez Elementary that supported students to look beyond popular science fair experiments to create social science projects with potential insight into academic challenges impacting people of color.

The ability to teach a content area and bring in relevant examples to connect with young people is challenging. With each employee hired, the desire and ability to create culturally responsive lesson plans guided every decision. Steinsberg acknowledged the hiring challenges of Marcus Chavez Elementary in the following comment,

> the hiring process has been especially interesting because you really want to hire socially conscious educators who also have the ability to teach the kids strong academic skills. The last thing we want is someone just talking all *Dangerous Mind* style with the kids and they don't learn anything. That's not what we want. We don't think it's enough to be an awesome math teacher. It's important to also have that social justice piece.

As Steinsberg acknowledged, the skill to provide a robust academic experience coupled with social justice awareness was integral to the success of the school. It went beyond fictional depictions resembling the 1995 film *Dangerous Minds*, where Michelle Pfeiffer portrays an empathetic high school teacher who accepts a position to educate a group of underserved students. Although Steinsberg, did not offer specific insight into how potential teachers were selected, from his words we can understand that hiring and retention decisions were assessed on an individual's abilities to teach a subject such as math and incorporate critical discussions on topics relevant to the students' lives.

As I continued to speak with Mr. Steinsberg, I wanted to hear more about the benefits and challenges of serving as an administrator or teacher at Marcus Chavez Elementary. I presented the question, "what are the benefits of working at MCE?" He replied, "I think the benefits of being a teacher at MCE is that things such as a child's social-emotional development, identity, and character is considered of high importance. There isn't only an academic focus that you may see at other schools. The principal really does value educating the whole person." Mr. Steinsberg spoke to the emphasis on "social-emotional development, identity, and character" that is intrinsic to the work at Marcus Chavez Elementary. The ability to meet the academic needs and other criteria is important to educating "the whole person." Steinsberg credits a significant portion of the school culture to the principal's leadership.

Although Marcus Chavez Elementary does an excellent job of supporting a culturally responsive curriculum and students' full development, there exists space for some necessary changes. When I asked Mr. Steinsberg about some of the challenges he said,

> Communication has always been a problem here at the school. People are doing so many things that messages get lost and communication is not as formulaic. The principal sometimes says yes to initiatives at the last minute and that makes things difficult for routines. So, for example, we will get an opportunity to attend an art thing. The principal will say yes, and we need to call every parent before tomorrow. It's exciting and frustrating.

As Steinsberg notes, communication at Marcus Chavez Elementary was an area in need of improvement. In a passion-filled environment such as Marcus Chavez Elementary, I observed occasions when decisions were made without regard for protocol or group consensus. Teachers and administrators were mandated to complete tasks that were dream opportunities for students, but a nightmare for the adults responsible for organization and management.

# A Teacher's Application

Ms. Osuna, a Latina from a Mexican background, was a twenty-seven-year-old second year teacher. She served as one of the lead teachers in the Politics 100 course and organizers in the student led march to the juvenile detention center. To gain an understanding of how she interpreted culturally responsive curriculum and her experiences as an educator at Marcus Chavez Elementary, I asked her to participate in an interview during one of her scheduled prep times of the day. Without hesitation, she agreed to sit down with me and offer her insights to the students, staff, curriculum, and other components of the school.

I began by asking Ms. Osuna about what she knew about the school's conception. She said,

> The story that I was told was that, the principal and her mother first started a day-care on the Westside of Chicago and the students were leaving and going to public schools. They were not doing as well in the CPS schools. So, they [the principal and manager] decided to create their own school where the curriculum matched what they saw as vital. It was really about supporting a majority Black student population, but also some Brown students.

From Ms. Osuna's understanding of how the school began, Marcus Chavez Elementary started in response to evidence that students of color possessed limited quality public school options. The decision to use a culturally responsive curriculum and correct some of the inadequacies of public schools influenced the principal and manager to open Marcus Chavez Elementary.

When I asked Ms. Osuna about how she saw the school could change in ten years, her response offered a glimpse into the current state of affairs at the school and how she envisioned the future. "I see MCE having a much larger student population. I think in its beginning the class sizes were small and intentional. But now, I think we are getting like twenty students to a room. Compared to CPS it's still not that much. For example, my class has only thirteen students, and I believe that is the last generation of those small classes. You know, going forward it is going to grow." In Ms. Osuna's words, she predicts the school "having a much larger student population." She believed in the vision at Marcus Chavez Elementary and witnessed the benefits that students experienced when compared with other Chicago school options.

To explore the social justice and culturally responsive components of the curriculum at Marcus Chavez Elementary, I asked Ms. Osuna to speak to the structure of Politics 100. Replacing the teachers' names with pseud-onyms, she said,

> Each homeroom has a campaign, and we basically decide with the students what social issue we are going to focus on for the year. So, for example, Ms. Santiago's class which is fifth grade they are doing bullying. Ms. Smith which is seventh/eighth they are teen pregnancy and my class sixth/seventh they decided to focus on sexual violence. We've been mainly focusing on child sexual abuse and the ways we can help prevent it or the ways we can support child victims. I want them to understand that child victims can look any sort of way. It affects all genders and ages.

From Ms. Osuna's comments, it is interpretable to extract she is passionate about the Politics 100 course. Not only is she able to speak to the content of her group, but she can also offer insight into the topics of other classes.

Intersectionality asks that we explore connections between multiple identities and phenomena. It is crucial to highlight Ms. Osuna's plea to create an intersectional analysis of sexual assault through her remarks, "I want them to understand that child victims can look any sort of way. It affects all gender and ages." The socially constructed identities of race, gender, age, and sexual orientation, influences perspectives and opportunities; they can serve as espe-cially salient lenses among adolescent Black males (Collins, 1999; Dottolo & Stewart, 2008; Ghavami & Peplau, 2013; Rogers, Scott, & Way, 2015; Shields, 2008). Through Ms. Osuna's comments coupled with Michael and Steve's acknowledgments in the previous chapter that sexual assault impacts boys and girls, it is feasible to suggest that intersectionality influenced peda-gogy at Marcus Chavez Elementary.

With an intention to demonstrate how socially constructed identities influence inequalities, teachers created lesson plans that were an intentional resource to highlight the experiences of racialized people. Ms. Osuna talked about her efforts to create awareness of the African diaspora.

> The units are all built on a different continent. So, we started with Africa, then we went to Latin America. Then we went to North America, and now we are in Asia. Next, will be Europe. I knew that going into each unit, it was still going to focus on Blackness. Africa was easy, but others were challenging. For example, with Asia and our focus on India, I wanted to make sure they understood there was a Black popula-tion living in that country. I wanted to show examples of the Black or rather African population. With Latin America, I talked about Afro Latinos and how that regardless of what country you are from, you can face racism because of your skin color.

In each of the units that investigated different world cultures and histories, Ms. Osuna made it a priority to reflect the backgrounds of the students.

As Ms. Osuna further discussed, it was challenging to create lesson plans that adequately covered the goals of each unit without imposing her opinions on the students. In our conversation she shared,

> I try to talk about how colonization affects Black people all over the world. It's also hard to have a conversation about colonization because I don't want to make Europeans sound inherently evil. It's hard! For example, in Africa, we know slavery existed before they came. But when Europeans came, they took that concept and did the most. They did unheard stuff with it, and it's hard not to demonize their behaviors. I want my students to understand that there was resistance. I'm working in my practice to show the narrative and demonstrate how people fought back.

It was challenging for Ms. Osuna to teach the students an unbiased version of European colonization. As a person of color who researched slavery in Africa, she understood the legacy of White supremacy and desired to share an accurate historical interpretation with her students that empowered them to shape their perspectives.

As a Latina with a fairer skin complexion, she talked about the students' perceptions of her race.

> When students say things about not trusting White people, I validate their opinions given the context of our classroom discussions on colonization. I understand how they might not trust me as someone who is White passing. I have not trusted others who look like they are White. I get it. I think early on they [students] asked what I was. I think that because of my name they knew that I wasn't White. You know like, I was intentional about sharing my background with them.

Ms. Osuna is a teacher, "who is White passing," and identifies as Latina. Aligned with critical race theory, she used her classroom to recognize the cultural capital of her identity and over time gained credibility as a person of color who encountered challenges with trusting people self-identified as White.

To tackle the essential topics identified in Politics 100, I was curious about how she structured her lesson plans and if an administrator gave her feedback. My question was, "in terms of your lesson plans, do you have complete authority of that or does someone check your lesson? How does that work?" Ms. Osuna responded, "they do check it. Our lesson plans are due on Sunday night, and one of the administrators checks them to make sure they are complete. But, I can basically do whatever I want to do." Ms. Osuna confirmed that lesson plans are collected to determine if teachers are attempting to meet curriculum objectives. She also declared autonomy by stating, "I can basically do whatever I want."

I probed further to determine the level of accountability in place to ensure teachers met the culturally responsive curriculum objectives identified in the school's mission. My question to Ms. Osuna was, "does anyone offer you feedback or is just that someone says, you're good, do what you do?" She responded,

> Steinsberg used to be really good about giving me feedback once a week. He would come by my classroom, observe, and then we would meet and discuss the lesson. That was good, but it's not happening as much anymore. Now, for the most part, my lesson plans are accepted on honor. [When the school year began], I did receive a framework for Politics 100 and some prior lesson plans, but for the most part I have to make everything up. I wish that I could get evaluated once a week. I appreciate the freedom, but I sometimes feel lost.

In Ms. Osuna's response, it is possible to hear that while she appreciates the autonomy to create lesson plans without supervision, it is also important to receive guidance. As a private independent school, Marcus Chavez Elementary was not concerned about standardized testing performance which enabled the instructional freedom discussed by Osuna. To some this relaxed environment of accountability is a benefit. It is also important to recognize that the school often did not offer the critical feedback necessary for growth as an educator.

To explore the benefits from Ms. Osuna's perspective about working at Marcus Chavez Elementary, I asked her to identify the positive components of the school. She stated,

> I love everyone who works here. I love my coworkers. I love the way that we just uplift Black and Brown people. I love the activism and that everything is focused on social justice. In my last job, no one ever mentioned race.

I asked about her previous job. She worked for a non-profit organization that offered a variety of services to people from lower income communities in Chicago. A component of the work she did with her former employer included teaching K-12 students in public schools. As her comment reveals, the non-profit organization she worked with was not explicit in the same ways that Marcus Chavez Elementary declared in their commitments to social justice and culturally responsive curricula for students of color.

Ms. Osuna continued to expand about the positive attributes that accompanied working with a group of similarly minded educators. She stated,

> I know that some of the students complain every day about the school, but they just don't know how good they have it. The stuff they are learning and the ways that all

the teachers try to be creative and really engaging while focusing on their identities is unique. We try to make things relevant to who they are and their lived experiences. It's a lot and I love being in this environment.

Ms. Osuna speaks to how some students may "complain about the school every day," and she affirms that the school culture is "unique" and valuable. In alignment with the objectives of culturally responsive curriculum theory and practice, she states "we [the staff] try to make things relevant to who they are and their lived experiences."

Despite Ms. Osuna's use of the word, "love," in multiple parts of her response to my question about the benefits of working at Marcus Chavez Elementary, I was also aware of some challenges. I asked, "what would you say is a drawback or a challenge from working here?" For clarification, I added, "your response doesn't have to include references to your teaching experiences. I want you to think about some of the difficulties that come with working at this school." Ms. Osuna took a moment to process my question and statement, before offering her a critical assessment of the environment at Marcus Chavez Elementary school.

After some thought, Ms. Osuna talked about feeling overwhelmed with her multiple responsibilities at the school.

> Sometimes, I feel like really at capacity. We not only have to do lesson plans and teach from 8 AM to four o'clock. We have to serve on committees and organize events. For example, the teachers were responsible for that last event. I mean really big events that we have to be in charge of after teaching or while we are teaching. With the teaching component, our prep time gets taken away to organize for events.

As an attendee at the school's "last event" which was a production of *The Lion King*, I understood Ms. Osuna's perspective. Teachers were made responsible for every component of an elaborate school musical and worked long hours to ensure it was successful. From my relationship with the school, I affirmed Ms. Osuna's comments about the long work days necessary to coordinate special events.

To bring the conversation back to the curriculum I asked Ms. Osuna, "how do you believe the curriculum is impacting the students and their communities." She clarified my question with one of her own, "do you mean specifically to social justice? I responded, "yes," and then she talked in detail about her observations.

> I think especially with our first unit, "all about me," I spent a lot of time talking about systemic oppression. I think it's giving them the language to discuss things they've

known about for a long time. They've known racism, sexism, homophobia, and all these things because even as a young person you see and hear these things all the time. When we talk about history, it gives them a connection to their ancestors. I hope it does. I have never heard anyone say that explicitly, but I hope the wheels are turning in their head and they are making the connection.

Ms. Osuna is hopeful that the lesson plans included as part of Politics 100 and other subjects taught at Marcus Chavez Elementary arm the students with the vocabulary to articulate and influence social inequalities. She mentions, "racism, sexism, and homophobia" as examples of the topics addressed in her classroom.

As Ms. Osuna continued to speak to the school culture, she helped foster with the students, teachers, and administrators of Marcus Chavez Elementary she remembered an incident that occurred earlier in the school year. She indicated,

> For example in my Latin America unit, we talked about the Spanish caste system and colorism. I talked about how colorism impact POC communities. I talked about how one Black person can feel something about another Black person based on skin color. Then, I can't remember if it was the same week, but one of my boys said that "he only likes girls with light skin." The girls responded "that's colorism. He is being a colorist." I wonder if I hadn't talked about colorism how they would have reacted to that statement. I don't know. Maybe they would have thought something, but not been able to vocalize it. I don't know.

As Ms. Osuna admitted, it is difficult to determine if the students' comments regarding colorism exemplified the effectiveness of her teachings. It is possible to speculate that the girls' choice in using "colorism" and "colorist" to describe the boy's comment about only liking "girls with light skin," reflects Ms. Osuna's discussion of the Spanish caste system.

## Capoeira and Beyond

The school culture that Mr. Steinsberg and Ms. Osuna articulated during their interviews is integral to understanding how Capoeira transitioned from a gym class to an after-school program aimed to increase positive self-awareness and inspire youth to impact social justice causes. Administration at Marcus Chavez Elementary supported Capoeira as a physical education class, because of the health benefits associated with consistent practice and the connection to the enslavement of African people. As Ms. Osuna discussed, teachers were intentional in their lesson plans to emphasize the experiences of the Black and Brown student population. Through Capoeira's roots in resistance movements of Brazil, I found it suitable with the support of the administration and teachers to use Capoeira as a resource to equip the students' bodies and minds.

As explored in the previous chapter, each session of the Capoeira program began with a discussion in the circle, roda. We talked about the students' experiences at school and the topics explored in courses such as Politics 100. When I worked at Marcus Chavez Elementary school as the gym teacher, I saw myself as one of the students' mentors. In the after-school program as a facilitator and researcher, I used the roda to continue mentorship, create new relationships, collect data, and to teach Capoeira. Together we used Capoeira as a resource to engage in a protest against police brutality.

Similar to any adult who decides to work with young people in the capacity of a teacher, counselor, administrator or another role, some challenges are inevitable. On multiple occasions, I was unable to have meaningful discussions with the students due to my inability to get them to focus their attention on the topic. When I began teaching Capoeira at Marcus Chavez Elementary, the first lesson the students taught me included the need for me to talk less and do more physical activity. I discovered that if I could explain the components of Capoeira's history while also getting them to move, I encountered fewer interruptions.

In alignment with youth development theory, I saw my role as a guide to the children in their journey from adolescence to adulthood. Recognizing their identities and equipping them with positive self-awareness remained a priority in each Capoeira class. Ms. Osuna and Mr. Steinsberg's interviews indicated how affirmation of the students' identities was integral in the academic subjects also. As documented in video clips, I talked to the students about race, gender, and sexual orientation discrimination. We also discussed their environments and the resources available to them, their friends, family, and others.

I shared with the students how race influenced the origins of Capoeira and continued to impact people today. We discussed slavery in Brazil and how post-emancipation race influenced the myriad ways Black people who practiced Capoeira became criminalized and ostracized. Many of my students only knew Chicago and lived in segregated underserved Black and Latinx communities. In alignment with the school culture at Marcus Chavez Elementary and classrooms similar to Ms. Osuna, I felt encouraged also to frame discussions relative to problems they identified in their communities.

We talked about violence, racism, systemic oppression, academic success, non-limiting belief systems, and other topics that corresponded with their identities. The school culture, as affirmed by Mr. Steinsberg and Ms. Osuna's comments, enabled our explorations of race and the legacy of White supremacy. Conversations about violence in their communities, the police shootings of Michael Brown, Rekia Boyd, and others were not easy to have but were a necessary component to extend Capoeira beyond self-defense movements, acrobatics, rituals, and music. I also encouraged the students to do their best in school, make positive contributions to their communities, and to make decisions from a well-informed stance.

The philosophies of Capoeira were aligned with the school's culturally responsive curriculum. For example, I talked about how the objectives inside some Capoeira games to not hit the other person is reflective of philosophies that support harmony rather than conflict. I told my students, it is an exercise in self-control to train the martial art movements without hitting the other person. This ability to practice without hurting their partner was valued among enslaved Africans, because it enabled the preservation of comrades necessary to fight a common oppressor. My goal was not to teach passive resistance but to build community and help the students understand the importance of limiting the power of their emotions to control their physical behaviors.

Although Capoeira is useful as a style of fighting, I made the self-defense application of movements a secondary goal of the after-school program. Yes, we trained the physical components of Capoeira in every class. We also explored social justice topics that included police shootings, environmental racism, and other issues consistent with the school culture created by the students, Mr. Steinsberg, Ms. Osuna, and other members of the staff. In the after-school program, a significant goal of mine included offering the best instructional practices to encourage positive self-awareness and contributions toward social justice movements. My work was only made possible by a supportive school culture that created classes like Politics 100 to investigate community challenges, propose solutions, and pursue remedies.

Although none of The Fellas spoke as leaders during the pre-rally, I took pride in knowing that they decided to attend and participate in other ways. We walked together in unison to challenge injustices against Black bodies in the United States. When the protest leaders called, we responded together. Through the conversations, we shared in class and their presence at the protest, I found evidence that the topics resonated with how Michael, Steve,

Jermaine, Jeff, and Wesley viewed themselves, their communities, and their potential to influence change.

To view footage from the march, and Capoeira classes visit: www.vlindsayphd.com/gallery

# Note

1. Pseudonyms were assigned to each of the teaching and administrative personnel to protect their identities.

# References

Bradley, M. S., Pulphus, J., & Jones, J. (2015). Ferguson, USA: A scholar's unforeseen connection and collision with history. *The Western Journal of Black Studies*, 39(4), 273–280.

Byrd, C. M., & Chavous, T. M. (2009). Racial identity and academic achievement in the neighborhood context: A multilevel analysis. *Journal of Youth and Adolescence*, 38(4), 544–559.

Collins, P. H. (1999). Moving beyond gender: Intersectionality and scientific knowledge. In M. F. Ferree, J. Lorber, & B. B. Hess (Eds.), *Revisioning gender* (pp. 261–284). Thousand Oaks, CA: Sage

Dottolo, A. L., & Stewart, A. J. (2008). "Don't ever forget now, you're a Black man in America": Intersections of race, class and gender in encounters with the police. *Sex Roles*, 59(5), 350–364.

Gay, G. (2000). *Culturally responsive teaching: Theory, research, and practice*. New York, NY: Teachers College Press.

Ghavami, N., & Peplau, L. A. (2013). An intersectional analysis of gender and ethnic stereotypes: Testing three hypotheses. *Psychology of Women Quarterly*, 37, 113–127.

Irvine-Jordan, J. (1991). *Black students and school failure: Policies, practices, and prescriptions*. New York, NY: Praeger Press.

Lowery, W. (2016). *They can't kill us all: Ferguson, Baltimore, and a New Era in America's Racial Justice Movement*. New York, NY: Little Brown and Company.

Murry, V. M., Berkel, C., Gaylord-Harden, N. K., Copeland-Linder, N., & Nation, M. (2011). Neighborhood poverty and adolescent development. *Journal of Research on Adolescence*, 21, 114–128.

Rogers, L. O., Scott, M. A., & Way, N. (2015). Racial and gender identity among black adolescent males: An intersectionality perspective. *Child Development*, 86(2), 407–424.

Sampson, D., & Garrison-Wade, F. D. (2011). Cultural vibrancy: Exploring the preferences of African American children toward culturally relevant and non-culturally relevant lessons. *Urban Review*, 43(2), 279–309.

Shields, S. A. (2008). Gender: An intersectionality perspective. *Sex Roles*, 59, 301–311.

Simpson, D., Bruckheimer, J., (Producers) & Smith, N. J. (Director). (1995). *Dangerous Minds* [Motion Picture]. United States: Hollywood Pictures and Don Simpson/Jerry Bruckheimer Films Via Rose Productions.

Smith, E. P., Atkins, J., & Connell, C. M. (2003). Family, school, and community factors and relationships to racial-ethnic attitudes and academic achievement. *American Journal of Community Psychology, 32*(1–2), 159–173.

Smith, E. P., Witherspoon, D. P., & Osgood, W. D. (2017). Positive youth development among diverse racial-ethnic children: Quality afterschool contexts as developmental assets. *Child Development, 88*(4), 1063–1078.

Youngblade, L. M., Theokas, C., Schulenberg, J., Curry, L., Huang, I. C., & Novak, M. (2007). Risk and promotive factors in families, schools, and communities: A contextual model of positive youth development in adolescence. *Pediatrics, 119*(Suppl. 1), S47–S53.

# · 6 ·

# RELEVANCE WITHOUT COMPROMISE

Are we intentionally failing our children? I believe when we do not look for resources or use creativity to provide young people with an education relevant to their lives, the answer to that question is yes. While I support the necessity of academic markers to indicate achievement, it is imperative we also consider the significance of applicable knowledge that improves the lives of other people in need. The combination of Capoeira and a culturally responsive curriculum at Marcus Chavez Elementary empowered students to identify challenges within their communities, create and act on strategies designed to influence change.

Marcus Chavez Elementary is not a perfect institution. In this book, I shared the difficulties that teachers encountered with regards to unclear expectations from administrators and a heavy workload. I also revealed the problems I experienced as the gym teacher and after-school facilitator with students. This book did not present a perfect education environment equipped with a magic wand called Capoeira. It offered insight into a school that decided to use a culturally responsive curriculum in the core academic subjects, physical education, and after-school programming in response to perceptions of inadequate public school options.

Students who attend Marcus Chavez Elementary receive a unique experience unavailable to many young people of color who live in Chicago. Many of the public, private, and charter schools lack resources to offer students holistic educational experiences. Marcus Chavez Elementary school's international studies program that takes groups of students on an annual trip outside the United States is rather unprecedented. An administration that supported Capoeira as a focal gym activity, contrary to the dominant western sports of basketball, baseball, or football, also made this elementary school rare.

In this final brief chapter, I share the strengths, weaknesses, and suggestions for improvement of the research presented in this book. I offer these analyses with the intention that someone in the future will expand the scope of this study to make a positive impact on other institutions and students from underserved communities. This chapter begins with some personal accounts of my history in school discussed in detail with my first book *Critical Race Theory and Education for Black Males: When Pretty Boys Become Men*. I include these abbreviated experiences here because they establish the motivation behind completing this research, teaching Capoeira, and supporting culturally responsive curricular initiatives. My overarching goal for this chapter is to offer insight into potential educational policies and future research studies that desire to follow similar methodologies.

## School Experiences, Research Influences, and Admitted Biases

"I am bored." "I hate school." These two statements were my favorite responses when asked to describe my feelings about school. They remained the same from kindergarten until I graduated from high school (Lindsay, 2018). Similar to other Black males within my circle of friends, I perceived school as a requirement to live in my parents' home, not as a vehicle with the potential to lead me down the road to opportunities. In the K-8 schools I attended, my favorite subjects were gym and recess because they allowed me time to play with my friends. Capoeira did not exist as an after-school option for me.

During high school, my appreciation for the active and social components of the school day expanded. My favorite times of the school day grew to include lunch, the passing period between classes, gym, and dismissal. I attended public schools with strict discipline policies and classrooms where on any given day, the teacher's lesson plan included more time allocated to classroom management and less to instruction. The teaching of math, science, language arts, and other subjects appeared secondary to the objectives of making sure everyone sat in their seat and only talked when they raised their hands. I frequently felt that school was more about control and less about preparation for a successful and autonomous life.

Reflecting now through critical race, intersectionality, youth development, and culturally responsive curricular lenses, I can see the reasons that I did not enjoy school. Limited examples of positive Black historical figures, my performances of masculinity, and a perceived disconnect between academics and my life were significant influences on my perceptions of school. Yes, the K-12 public schools I attended fulfilled their annual Black history month obligations. They taught me about Dr. Martin Luther King, Jr., Rosa Parks, and other well-known contributors to the civil rights movement. I appreciated and admired such figures in history during February every single year. For the remaining eight months, however, I was in a constant love-hate relationship with school, because while I enjoyed the time with my classmates, I despised sitting in class and listening to my teachers. Overall, the culture of the schools that I attended did not foster a positive identity for me as a male looking to discover my place in society as a Black boy.

Suspensions and detentions are part of my K-12 school records because I did not feel fulfilled by what schools offered me in the form of education. In the sixth grade and high school, I was suspended for not following school policies. I missed homework assignments, fought my classmates, refused to wear my school identification card, and talked during class without raising my hand for permission. My behavior reflected a disconnect between the identity I was forming and the student my teachers were informing through a curriculum that supported White supremacy. I resisted and punishment soon followed.

My feelings of disregard for school were not related to my parents' educational levels. It was clear that my parents valued education because they finished college and instilled the importance of school in me and my five sisters. An example of my parents' dedication to education was the "homework first" rule which stated that the television had to remain off until school assignments were completed. If you chose to break this rule, and I often did, some form of physical or verbal punishment was imminent. My siblings and I were not physically abused to make sure we earned good grades and behaved in school. We were raised in a religious home with parents who were not afraid to put "the fear of God in children." Education was apparently important to my family, however, I did not see the experiences of a young Black boy from the Southside of Chicago reflective in the curricula.

My school experiences, family background, perspectives, and interests shaped the research conducted for this book. Feelings of not seeing enough of the positive contributions that people of African descent have made to society influenced my need to understand more about the curriculum in use at Marcus Chavez Elementary. My appreciation for gym class and dedication to Capoeira impacted how I analyzed the after-school program and the students' responses. Growing up in a home with parents who valued education, influenced the mentor relationships I formed with students and inspired the encouragement I offered to them during difficult moments. Without ignoring my identity and connection to the material, I aimed to use an objective stance when collecting and interpreting the data for this study.

The experiences I described as a young Black male in school and those gathered from my participants are reflective of a historical relationship between race, racism, gender, and education. By way of the African diaspora, we are an extension of the legacies of Frederick Douglass, Booker T. Washington, and other Black males who went to school in search of liberation. Beginning in slavery, Black men and women were denied the right to obtain an education. Legalized exclusion from the opportunities accessible through school established a foundation for contemporary school inadequacies that do not prepare many Black males for success in their lives. These are the perspectives that shaped my approach to this research and caused me to develop feelings of responsibility to help young Black boys who are lost in schools, searching to find themselves.

One of the potential shortcomings of this research is my relationship with the participants. I saw myself in them and that perspective influenced how I collected data. Instead of assuming the stance of an outsider and observing the subjects from a distance, I became a member of their community. The Fellas who participated in this study saw me as their teacher, mentor, brother, and friend. It is naïve to believe that our familiarity did not encourage more positive responses about Capoeira and about their experiences at Marcus Chavez Elementary.

The participants volunteered their time, and I did not coerce their responses or ask they support my beliefs about the significance of Capoeira and the culturally responsive curriculum. To my understanding, they were genuine in the activities of this research. I am also aware of the desire for approval that many boys look to receive from older men. In asking a graduate student who had less familiarity with the students to help gather data, I attempted to put an additional barrier in place to minimize my influence.

A duplicate study might explore additional strategies to reduce biases in the responses from their subjects.

I would like also to recognize that my relationship with school administrators and teachers impacted the data gathered for this study. Working with Marcus Chavez Elementary in various roles for six years before beginning this research put me in a unique position. The staff were comfortable with me and responded to my requests for interviews and observations without much hesitation. Although I shared the positive and negative aspects of my findings, it is undeniable that I am fond of the people and mission that influence the success of the site where I gathered research for this study.

When I began as the gym teacher at Marcus Chavez Elementary, it became clear that I had the support to create a unique program with Capoeira as a focal activity for gym class. I was granted the autonomy to form a physical education curriculum, with the only caveat to resemble the state standards for physical education in Illinois. Similar to the process Ms. Osuna described in chapter five, with lesson plan reviews, observations, and individual meetings, the administrators supported my development of a culturally responsive physical education curriculum for gym class. It is also important to acknowledge that the trip to Brazil at the end of the first year I taught Capoeira played a significant role in the popularity of the program that endured after the transition of my role as the gym teacher to an after-school facilitator.

## What about the Girls and Other Improvement Suggestions?

In future research, I encourage investigations that explore the voices of young people in schools who identify as girls and train Capoeira. As Dyson (2018) notes, we often focus on Black boys, while girls are being expelled from school at similar rates. The after-school program that provided data for this study did not exclude girls. From the beginning, when Capoeira served as the focal activity for gym class to the transition to an after-school program, I had the honor to teach students who identified as boys and girls. My female students were responsive to Capoeira and able to participate with the males. Indicated in the introductory chapter of this book are my reasons for highlighting the experiences of young men; however, I also found great value in the contributions of the young ladies in my classes.

In addition to the five boys who participated in this study, there exist three girls who also shared their viewpoints in interviews and granted permission for observations in class. In a future writing project, I will share their perspectives on the value of Capoeira and culturally responsive curriculum. They discussed a different set of factors that influenced their experiences at Marcus Chavez Elementary. Researchers, teachers, administrators, policymakers, and others can learn how to improve academic and social support resources in schools by listening to and observing students gendered as girls.

I would also add that future studies should highlight public schools that do not use a culturally responsive curriculum. Without question, the success of the Capoeira program and the research gathered is related to the Marcus Chavez Elementary school's status as a private independent school with the freedom and resources to establish a culture aligned with social justice. The administration could support Capoeira as physical education because they did not share the restrictions that often accompany public schools. Unlike other schools, neither the city school board nor the tax payers dictated the curriculum. The owners of the school, teachers, and parents determined the academic and other learning objectives of Marcus Chavez Elementary school students. Without conducting a similar study in a public school responsible for meeting external standards, it is difficult to determine whether the results reported in this study are replicable in other types of institutions.

## Implications for Policies and Beyond

The 45th US Presidency of Donald Trump is cause for alarm on multiple levels including the state of education in the United States. With Betsy DeVos' appointment as Secretary of Education, without prior academic administrative experience, there exists limited evidence that she will serve as an advocate for youth from lower-income communities (Green & Castro, 2017; Horsford, 2018; Toppo, 2016). At the time of this writing, Trump's administration has indicated and started the process to rescind Obama's efforts to create more opportunities through education; he has signed into law an act that establishes increased support for technical training (Burke & Jeffries, 2018; House, 2018; Ujifusa, 2018). During this era of an administration that openly advocates for policies supported by a racist, sexist, and xenophobic agenda, schools are an important resource for underserved populations.

Marcus Chavez Elementary is an institution designed to challenge the status quo. Through a culturally responsive curriculum, they equip students with the knowledge of themselves, the skills necessary for academic achievement, increased awareness of challenges facing their communities, and the courage to influence societal changes. My interviews with the students revealed how the course, Politics 100, enabled them to identify problems in their neighborhoods and to devise strategies aimed at creating solutions. Teachers and administrators confirmed how the school took alternative approaches not found in many public institutions, to prepare students for successes that transcended standardized tests and influenced social justice causes.

The Capoeira program was one of the initiatives unique to Marcus Chavez Elementary. As indicated in chapter three, it began as the center activity for the gym period, where kindergarten through third grade students took classes. With the school's growth, Capoeira classes expanded to include fourth through eighth grade students and an after-school initiative. The movements, music, philosophies, and rituals taught when Capoeira was offered as physical education were presented in alignment with the objectives of the culturally responsive curriculum created at the school.

Reflective of the findings presented in this research, more schools should make use of culturally responsive curricula to improve educational experiences for young people of color from underserved communities. The students and staff illustrated the significance of a curriculum that advocated for social justice. As Ms. Osuna confirmed, it is vital that administrators provide guidance and support in implementing a culturally responsive curriculum. Actions such as classroom observations and the encouragement of mentorships among staff will increase accountability and the development of robust curricula. Policies that mandate teachers to create lesson plans relative to the advantages and disadvantages that accompany living in their students' neighborhoods is a start at improving education.

Capoeira is a valuable resource that schools should also use to increase positive self-awareness, encourage academic achievement, and participate in social justice movements. Through sharing stories of Capoeira's origins among enslaved Africans in Brazil, it offers opportunities to increase students' awareness to the creativity, resistance, and resilience necessary to produce lasting success. By teaching the self-defense movements and having conversations about nutrition, it provides Black males and other youth with encouragement to live more active lives and make healthier lifestyle choices. For young people of African descent, it can provide another example in Black history of ancestors who equipped their bodies, minds, and spirits with the tools necessary to make unflinching strides toward freedom.

# Final Perspectives

Limited economic opportunities, high rates of homicide, and the overrepresentation of Black males in prison can be tied to academic underachievement and the failures of schools to provide the resources necessary for life-long learning and achievement. Too often, Black boys attend schools where teachers make use of a curriculum that is not relevant to their lives. Without the practical skills of understanding their potential to create a viable business, pursue higher education, or find gainful employment, some Black males resort to illegal activities to provide for themselves and their families. At the root of these decisions is a school system that leads many students from underserved communities to prison or premature deaths. These claims are not conspiracy theories, but derivatives of flawed educational policies that underserve the interests and needs of people of color.

Black boys, other young people, and all adults should receive the full benefits of an education that connects the curriculum taught in school to tangible opportunities in the world. Whether it is finding a job, creating a business, receiving a college education, or pursuing an alternative career in the arts, schools should serve as the starting point for positive self-awareness and the acquisition of skills to unlock potential. A quality education should enable the development of social consciousness, courage, and the confidence among all students to analyze problems and create pathways toward solutions. It's unfortunate we live in a society where students' race, gender, and economic backgrounds influence the opportunities offered through the resources available in education.

Until we have remedied the problems that result from individual and systemic racism, conversations and other actions intended to impact social inequalities remain imperative. Without compromise, we must change academic curriculum and support after-school programs. In the Marcus Chavez Elementary school culture, I observed students, teachers, and administrators attempting to do their part in making positive progress toward a more just society. From the beginning of the day when Black males and other students arrive at school, to the after-school programs that spill into evening protests, we must maximize the resources to encourage academic achievement and social justice. Capoeira and culturally responsive curriculum can serve as key pieces to the puzzle known as freedom.

To read more of my writings on Capoeira, leadership, and social justice please subscribe to my blog at www.vlindsayphd.com/blog

# References

Burke, L. M., & Jeffries, S. (2018). Trump and the nation's schools—Assessing the administration's early impact on education. *Education Next, 18*(3), 58–65.

Dyson, M. E. (2018). *What truth sounds like: RFK, James Baldwin, and our unfinished conversation about race in America.* New York, NY: St. Martin's Press.

Green, T. L., & Castro, A. (2017). Doing counterwork in the age of a counterfeit president: Resisting a Trump–DeVos education agenda. *International Journal of Qualitative Studies in Education, 30*(10), 912–919.

Lindsay, V. (2018). *Critical race and education for black males: When pretty boys become men.* New York, NY: Peter Lang Press.

Horsford, S. D. (2018). Making America's schools great now: Reclaiming democracy and activist leadership under Trump. *Journal of Educational Administration and History, 50*(1), 3–11.

House-Education and the Workforce | Senate—Health, Education, Labor, and Pensions. (2018). *H.R.2353 – Strengthening career and technical education for the 21st century act: 115th congress (2017–2018).* Retrieved from https://www.congress.gov/bill/115th-congress/house-bill/2353

Toppo, G. (2016, November 23). 5 things to know about Trump's education secretary pick: Betsy DeVos. *USA Today.* Retrieved from https://www.usatoday.com/story/news/2016/11/23/5-things-know-trumps-education-secretary-pick-betsy-devos/94360110/

# APPENDIX

For Capoeira instructional videos, merchandise, and other resources visit:
www.vlindsayphd.com/capoeira

# A1. Focus Group Interview Questions

Although we ask everyone in the group to respect everyone's privacy and confidentiality, by not identifying anyone in the group or repeating what is said during the group discussion, please remember that other participants in the group may accidentally disclose what is said.

Probe: I want you to think about the problem that you talked about during your social justice and/or capoeira class.

1. What problem did you work on?
2. Why does the problem you have identified exist?
3. Who are the people who are most affected by the issue? Who benefited from the problem?
4. What was being done about the problem within your community?
5. How did you work with people in the community about the problem? How did you work with the leaders in the community?
6. How did you let other people in the community know about the problem?
7. What influence did you have with the people in charge?
8. What steps did you do as a class to take action? Who participated? Did you complete all of the steps on your plan?
9. What were the goals for your action? How do you know if you accomplished your goals?
10. What were the challenges? What could you have done better?
11. What else needs to be done about this problem in the future?
    - What other problems in the community need to be addressed? What are we going to do as a class to help the community reach this goal?
    - How did this impact the community? Help the community? Help people who were affected by the problem?
12. How did this impact you?
13. How does Capoeira impact you?

Updated Focus Group Questions v (3) 8/6/15

# A2. Student Individual Interview Questions

Although we ask everyone in the group to respect everyone's privacy and confidentiality, by not identifying anyone in the group or repeating what is said during the group discussion, please remember that other participants in the group may accidentally disclose what was said.

**Probe: Let's continue our discussion that we started in the focus group interview about the problem that was discussed in your social justice and/or capoeira class.**

1. What steps did you do as a class to take action? Who participated? Did you complete all of the steps on your plan?
2. What were the goals for your action? How do you know if you accomplished your goals?
3. What were the challenges? What could you have done better?
4. What else needs to be done about this problem in the future?
   –What other problems in the community need to be addressed?
   –What are we going to do as a class to help the community reach this goal?
5. How did this impact the community? Help the community? Help people who were affected by the problem?
6. How does Capoeira impact you?
7. Do you see Capoeira as something that can help you address a problem in your community?

Updated Individual Interviews version (2) 8/6/15

# A3. Teacher/Administration Individual Interview Questions

**Probe:** I would like you to be frank with me about the history of MCE and what roles you served/currently serve in the development of curriculum.

1. Can you tell me about the history of MCE? How did the school start? How is it different today? Where do you see the school in 10 years?
2. What does culturally relevant curriculum mean to you?
3. How do you decide which materials are appropriate for your students? Who determines if your pedagogy is culturally relevant? How are students involved in the evaluation of curricula?
4. Do you have complete authority over lesson planning and the selection of classroom materials?
5. What are the benefits of being a teacher/administrator at MCE?
6. What are the setbacks of being employed at MCE?
7. How do you believe the curriculum is impacting MCE students?
8. How do you believe the curriculum is impacting the communities of MCE students?
9. What inspired you to pursue teaching/administration as a career? What continues to motivate you to return to work every day?

Teacher/Admin Individual Interviews version (1) 12/18/15

# A4. Capoeira Written Test

**Instructions: Please answer in complete sentences, fill in the bank, or circle the appropriate answer.**

1. Which instrument is said to "command the circle?"

   _____

   _____

2. Where is the Pandeiro originally from?
   A. Europe
   B. Brazil
   C. United States of America
   D. Antarctica
   E. East Afrika

3. The Atabaque is made of _____ and tightened by _____.

4. The Ago-go is used in Capoeira and what dance?
   A. The Jerk
   B. The Samba
   C. The Percolator
   D. The Jerk
   E. The Cabbage Patch

5. Older pandeiros are made from_____

6. What is tied to the ends of the Berimbau?

   _____

   _____

7. What is the basic hand pattern to play the Atabaque?
   A. left, left, right, right
   B. right, left, right, right
   C. right, left, right, left
   D. left, right, right, right

8. Why did Africans use instruments in their training of Capoeira?

_____

_____

_____

_____

## A5. Capoeira Lesson Plan

Teacher Name ___ Vernon Lindsay ___
Weekly Unit Planning Template

| Subj | | Monday | Tuesday | Wednesday | Thursday | Friday |
|---|---|---|---|---|---|---|
| Capoeira | **UNIT** | **Unit Learning Objective(s):** Sequencia; develop physical movements. **IL Learning Standard(s): State Goals 19-A.** Follow directions and class procedures while participating in physical activities. B. Work cooperatively with another to accomplish an assigned task. C. Work independently on tasks for short periods of time. **Overview:** Students will learn a new song and I will introduce a kick to enhance movements of Capoeira. **Vocabulary:** Armada, Sequencia, Balancia, Ginga, Berimbau, Aú, Ponche, South America, Afrika, Angola, Brasil, Banaderia **Assessment:** Students will be asked to demonstrate sequence inside of roda | | | | |
| | **LESSONS** | Lesson Goal(s): 1. New Song 2. Sequencia 3. Develop movements  Description: 1. Music 2. Warm up 3. Sequencia Movements 4. Armada 5. Stretch and cool down  Assessment: Roda | Lesson Goal(s): Description: Assessment: | Lesson Goal(s): 1. Music comprehension 2. Develop Balancia  Description: 1. Music 2. Warm up 3. Sequencia 4. Armada 5. Stretch and cool down  Assessment: Roda | Lesson Goal(s): Description: Assessment: | Lesson Goal(s): 2. The Sequencia Roda!  Description: 1. Warm up 2. Stretch 3. Sequencia Roda 4. Stretch and cool down  Assessment: Roda |

# A6.  Student's Capoeira In-class Test

2.   Mestre Bimba's mother's name was

   A.  Beyonce

   B.  Ciara

   C.  Janet Jackson

   D.  Niki Minaj

   E.  Dona Maria Martinha

3.  Manoel dos Reis Machado was Mestre's Bimba's birth name T/F

4.  Mestre Bimba was the first to provide his students with cords T/F

5.  Mestre Bimba died

   A.  January 6, 2011

   B.  January 31, 2010

   C.  February 5, 1974

   D.  April 8, 2011

**Short Answer: Answer the questions with a complete sentence or two (15 pts)**

6.  Why do you think Mestre Bimba discouraged his students from participating in street rodas? *Because it would not be fun or harmful, and not*

7.  What was Bimbas' purpose for providing students cords? *Recognition of different ... within*

8.  Why do you believe Mestre Bimba discouraged his students from participating in street rodas? *Because he ... is not safe*

**Bonus Question: (10 pts)**

What style of Capoeira is practiced at our school? *... African ogee and ca ...*

# A7. Capoeira Gym Class Assignment

Name:_____
Date:_____

Instructor Lindsay

Capoeira training
week of Sept 13

**Directions:** Do these Capoeira exercises with the supervision of your parent/guardian or designated adult. These exercises should be done at least three days per week. Be sure to drink water as needed in between exercises (6–8 ounces every 15 minutes). This signed assignment is due every MONDAY at the start of class.

**Exercises should be completed in this order:**
1. 2 sets of **15 pushups**
2. 2 sets of **15 sit ups**

3. **Ginga** for **5** minutes without stopping (remember to protect your face and keep a low stance)
4. Warm up **stretch**
5. **10 Meia-lua de frente** (front step kick)—outside to inside half moon kick
6. **10 Mei-lua de frente** (back leg)—outside to inside half moon kick
7. **10 Cocorinha esquivas**—squat with feet flat on ground and hand up but not blocking face from potential incoming attacks.
8. **Stretch** all major muscle groups

**Please circle the days that these exercises were completed:**

Sunday   Monday   Tuesday   Wednesday   Thursday   Friday   Saturday

I witnessed _____ complete the Capoeira training required for this week:
Relationship to child: _____
Printed Name and Signature: _____

## A8.  Capoeira Instrument Test

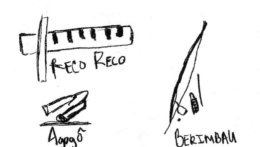

# A9. Capoeira Parent Letter

Dear Parent/Guardian:                                      September 13, 2010

We are at the start of another year at _____ and beginning a new season of
Capoeira! For our new parent(s)/guardian(s), Capoeira is an African-Brazilian martial art
form that combines elements of music, song, dance, and gymnastics with self-defense.
Students learn self-defense tactics, acrobatics, how to play instruments and sing in
Portuguese as participants in the Capoeira Roda (pronounced Hor-A), where all the
elements of the martial art meet. Enslaved Africans developed Capoeira as a tool to fight
their captors, so when they trained they did so in a manner where they did not aim to hurt
each other. At_____, we continue this legacy of training without intentions to harm
one another. Capoeira serves as a vehicle to build relationships and celebrate
commonalities across our communities.

In continuing with the success of _____, I aim to help develop your
student's Capoeira skills and overall physical health. Your student will participate in
Capoeira class on Mondays and Wednesdays at _____ as a part of the
physical education curriculum. Second, third and fourth grade classes have the added
responsibility to maintain a Capoeira journal and home training schedule. Students are
required to bring journals to class and take notes on movements, philosophy, songs,
struggles with Capoeira, etc. Any 70 page notebook will suffice for use as a Capoeira
journal; if you have difficulty purchasing a notebook, one will be purchased for your
student. The training schedule is a weekly assignment that requires the student to
complete Capoeira movements under the supervision of an adult. Schedules should be
signed and returned to class every Monday; whereas the Capoeira journal will be checked
at random twice throughout the quarter. The Capoeira journal and training schedules are
mandatory homework assignments that will help build discipline, honesty, responsibility
and an investment in their overall physical health. These assignments will be configured
into their final grade. I appreciate your support in this new endeavor.

Please sign and return the following page, provide emergency contact information and
add any comments by Wednesday September 15, 2010. Please feel free to contact me
with any questions via email .

Emergency Contact information:

Student Name:_____

Parent/ Guardian Name:_____

Relationship to student:_____

Phone: _____

Comments:

Printed Name: _____
Parent/guardian signature: _____

Thank you for your time and assistance with Capoeira,

Sincerely,

Instructor Lindsay

# A10. Student Homework Sample Response

Name
Date: _2 -5-11_
Grade: _GR_

Instructor Lindsay

Capoeira training week of Jan 31

**Directions: Do these Capoeira exercises with the supervision of your parent/guardian or designated adult. These exercises should be done at least two days per week. Be sure to drink water as needed in between exercises (6-8 ounces every 15 minutes). This signed assignment is due every MONDAY at the start of class.**

**Exercises should be completed in this order:**

1. 2 sets of **15 pushups**

2. 2 sets of **15 sit ups**

3. **Ginga** for **5** minutes without stopping (remember to protect your face and keep a low stance)

4. Warm up **stretch**

5. **20 Armada ( R-Ma-Da)[10- left (esquerda) and 10 right (direito)| - spinning crescent kick 1. Step um dois 2. Look over your shoulder and see your target 3. Back leg kicks**

*__*hint- if you look over your left shoulder, left leg will kick; if you look over your right shoulder, right leg will kick__*

6. **Stretch** all major muscle groups

**Please circle two days that these exercises were completed:**

Sunday    Monday    Tuesday    Wednesday    Thursday    Friday    Saturday
I witnessed

complete the Capoeira training required for this week:

(student name)
Relationship to child: _Father_

Printed Name:

Parent signature:

*All identifiable information has been removed from the document

# INDEX

**GLOBAL
INTERSECTIONALITY
OF EDUCATION, SPORTS,
RACE, AND GENDER**

Billy Hawkins, *General Editor*

The Global Intersectionality of Education, Sports, Race, and Gender series responds to the interesting dialogue and unique social phenomena in the global context produced by the intersections of race, sport, gender, and culture. Global Intersectionality explores these intersections and expands the literature on how each inform our thinking around certain dominant ideologies. This series examines how sporting practices in the United States are becoming the global norm in defining what is sport, thus our understanding of race, gender, and culture.

The purpose of this series is to inform sport enthusiasts, college students, educators, researchers, policy makers, and other stakeholders—who are social justice oriented—about the role sport has in contributing to informing cultural ideology, reproducing and reinforcing race and gender ideologies. It also seeks to foster an understanding of how this social phenomenon, that is often situated as merely entertainment or a recreational activity for leisure, has shifted into a cultural practice that can engender global socio-political relations. The topics will include critical moments in sport, as well as broader social movements in sporting context. In addition, this series will discuss topics ranging from youth to professional sporting experiences with attention given to the socialization and educational processes inherent in these experiences as it relates to race, gender, and culture.

Titles in this series will employ a variety of methodologies, including, but not limited to, qualitative, quantitative, mixed methods methodological approaches, non-empirical and socio-historical approaches that incorporate primary and secondary data sources. For additional information about this series or for the submission of manuscripts, please contact:

Peter Lang Publishing. Inc.
Acquisitions Department
29 Broadway, 18th Floor
New York, NY 10006

To order other books in this series, please contact our Customer Service Department:

(800) 770-LANG (within the U.S.) | (212) 647-7706 (outside the U.S.)
(212) 647-7707 FAX

Or browse online by series: www.peterlang.com

www.ingramcontent.com/pod-product-compliance
Lightning Source LLC
Chambersburg PA
CBHW070949050326
40689CB00014B/3404